100 Fun Ways to Teach the Bible to Children

compiled by

CATHY KYTE

EASTBOURNE

Other titles in this series:

Dedicated to
Ben, Andrew & Joanna

thanks for all the great times
of fun and laughter

Unless otherwise indicated, biblical quotations
are from the New International Version © 1973, 1978, 1984
by the International Bible Society.

ISBN 1 - 84291 - 127 - 9
Published by Kingsway Communications Ltd,
26 Lottbridge Drove, Eastbourne,
East Sussex BN23 6NT

Cover design and production for the publishers by
Bookprint Creative Services,
P.O. Box 827, BN21 3YJ, England.
Printed in Great Britain.

Contents

Acknowledgements

This book is a testimony to teamwork, co-operation and the various skills and specialities of the people who represent Children's Ministry.

Originally, I devised a seminar on the topic for our Children's Ministry training days, where children's workers gather to receive input and inspiration. We soon recognized that a record of this seminar – expanded and developed – would be a great resource.

So with the invaluable help of Ruth Alliston and Andy Back, we began to compile a list of suitable stories and memory verses under each age group. Andy continued by spearheading the project, drawing the contents together and writing the introduction. He also wrote, along with Jenny Brown, the entries for the 9-13s section. Ruth's contribution was enormous, providing nearly all of the rest of the entries, writing with her inimitable charm for under 5s and for 5-9s, and making use of some materials written by Sue Price.

And then with the energy and enthusiasm of Ruth Price, the whole project took shape and the book was brought to life.

So while it may be my name on the cover, I am very grateful to my friends (much more than colleagues!) for helping put this resource into your hands.

Cathy Kyte, Wimbledon, June 2003

Introduction
by Andy Back

When I consider my Christian education, I remember most vividly the characters. It was a while ago, when boys were boys and Sunday school teachers were respected, and when we were brought up properly and addressed them politely. I am pleased to acknowledge Mr Osborne, Mrs Goodchild and Mr Elkin.

Each poured their lives into mine, taking trouble to ensure that I learned Bible truth and not just their opinions. I am so grateful that God brought these heroes of the faith across my path.

Stories for life

They did their best to captivate my attention, my interest and my heart with the good news of the gospel and how to life a Christian life according to Bible principles. Their styles varied, but each had a way of winning me over from distractions, youthful exuberance and the myriad other things that filled my head.

They used such diversions as music, shouts, odd spots (object lessons), crafts, discussion, games, activities, demonstrations, posters, films – all sorts of ways of connecting with me and capturing my attention and interest. Even way back then, these faithful workers had realized that if they made Bible stories fun, they would have so much more success in trying to teach us. They also tried to have sessions that were not just a chore for them to get through, but a pleasant experience for all.

I am passionate about the stories of the Bible and for the ways they relate to my circumstances and can be applied to my life. This is rooted, I am sure, in the creative way in which the stories were communicated to me.

Trying to remember

Back then, of course, memory verses were not a forgotten art. They were fading fast as a regular aspect of the sessions, but I'm sure I won a prize for scripture recall, having committed a dozen or more Authorized Version texts to memory. Wist thee, or canst thou not?

Joking apart, I'm glad that competition had a lasting positive effect upon me, equipping my spirit with tools to help me walk in the light.

The key to memorisation is, of course, repetition. There is no getting around this, and there are no short cuts, since the way the connections are formed in the brain is through familiarity. Consider for a moment: can you remember the words to the second verse of the National Anthem? No?

What about the second verse of *While Shepherds Watched their Flocks by Night*? I'd guess you can!

The difference, of course, is that while we may only sing Christmas Carols in December each year, and even then just a couple of times each, this repetition is sufficient to reinforce connections made a long time before. If you knew the next verse began *'Fear not' said he, for mighty dread / Had seized their troubled minds,* then those connections deep inside your head are still there, no matter how long it may be since you last had to call upon them. They have been repeated enough times to make them relatively permanent fixtures. The trouble with the second verse of the National Anthem is that we almost never sing it, or even hear it being sung, so the connections haven't been made.*

A friend of mine testified that she was required to learn a poem (I think it was one by Walter de la Mare) when she was at school, which was a considerable time ago. A gentleman does not even speculate about how long ago it might have been, but for the purposes of this illustration let's just agree that we are talking about a matter of about three decades, give or take a discretion or two. Anyway, the point is that after all this time she is still able to recite the poem she learned so long ago with confidence and without

---

* 2nd verse of the National Anthem: O Lord our God arise / Scatter our enemies / And make them fall! / Confound their knavish tricks / Confuse their politics / On you our hopes we fix / God save the Queen!

error. The process was so successful that even though she last recited the words when she was a schoolgirl, when she tried to recall the poem many... ahem, several years later, she was able to do so. You can read this story in more detail in the *Children's Ministry Guide to Tailored Teaching for 5-9s*.

Now, this is encouragement to us as we work to teach children to memorize scriptures. There are at least three advantages for us: we would not normally be memorizing long passages of poetry, but brief Bible verses. Secondly, we pray that the best part of thirty years will not elapse between learning and recalling. And since we are learning the word of God, we can expect some spiritual help!

Throughout the selection process for this book, we have worked hard to choose relevant, helpful and relatively short verses, knowing that the task of scripture memory is fairly time-consuming and energy-intensive even when there are just a small number of words to learn.

Having said this about short selections, I am so glad that when I was privileged to attend a school of evangelism, the godly team of tutors set us some Bible passages to learn. The process of learning Philippians 2:1-12 was a very worthwhile study of the grace and mercy of the Lord Jesus, laying down his glory and becoming a servant, obedient even unto death.

Memorizing is a matter of review, so whenever there was a spare moment in the day (riding on a bus, waiting for the kettle, standing in the supermarket checkout queue) I would work on this most excellent passage. After a little while, this eternal truth had become a part of me, and for all the years since, I have been able to rejoice in this praise poem about the unchanging, life-giving Saviour to whom every knee will bow, in heaven, on earth and under the earth.

I guess it's no accident that we call this 'learning by heart', as the activity is one which involves our emotional centre as well as our grey matter.

Now, it has to be said that I could have looked up Philippians 2 in my Bible at any time, but having the words at my fingertips gives me an advantage when the enemy tries to distract me or fill my mind with ungodly thoughts.

A biblical principle

Scripture memory is strongly encouraged in the Bible, for a number of good reasons.

> These commandments that I give you today are to be upon your hearts. Impress them on your children. Talk about them when you sit at home and when you walk along the road, when you lie down and when you get up. Tie them as symbols on your hands and bind them on your foreheads. Write them on the door-frames of your houses and on your gates. (Deuteronomy 6:6-9)

We may be quick to dismiss these sorts of commands as belonging to the old covenant. Hebrews carried phylacteries (boxes with little parchments with scriptures written on them) tied onto their heads and arms, and mounted a mezuzah (a tiny box holding further parchments) on their door-posts for the purpose of touching them as they entered or left the home. Surely God's intention was that his people carried his word in their hearts as well as on their clothes and door-posts.

The most important part of the command was to impress the Scripture upon children, to talk about the word of God in the home, irrespective of the job at hand or the time of day.

Consider the Lord Jesus in the wilderness, facing the Devil's temptations (Luke 4:1-13). Each time he is tempted, Jesus quotes Scripture (probably memorized when he was a child) and with these words of truth he defeats the father of lies.

A powerful weapon indeed! He avoids sin, and the enemy has to flee.

> I've hidden your word in my heart, that I might not sin against you.
> (Psalm 119:11)

King David obeyed the command in Deuteronomy, and had a good reason for doing so. He desired to walk in righteousness. Okay, so he wasn't entirely successful, but his attitude was right.

> Your word is a lamp to my feet and a light for my path.
> (Psalm 119:105)

How can we see the light if we do not know the word? Respect for the Scripture is explicit here; so let's take the trouble to commit it to memory, to teach it to our children, to meditate upon it and discuss it and learn from it and delight in it.

The trendy question *What Would Jesus Do?* can become just a pressurizing, guilt-inducing conundrum of little positive value unless we know enough of what Jesus did to be able to guess what he would do. What Jesus did most often, of course, was to do the will of the Father, discerned by the Holy Spirit. But that won't fit neatly on an embroidered wristband.

And then, of course, there is the best-known verse about the Bible in the Bible.

> All Scripture is God-breathed and is useful for teaching, rebuking, correcting and training in righteousness, so that the man of God may be thoroughly equipped for every good work.
>
> (2 Timothy 3:16,17)

Classically self-referential, these verses define why God has given us his Word – so that we can learn about him and his ways, be admonished for our sins, be shown the right way forward and develop our character into more Christlikeness. God desires that we are equipped for good works, and the Scriptures are provided to ensure we can be ready for action.

Since it is all inspired ('breathed') by God, it is all valid, worthy, correct and helpful, so we could just go ahead and choose any verses we like. But when we carefully select promises and encouragements which proceed from the mouth of God, we build ourselves up in our faith.

Helping us remember

The scriptures we can recall most easily are probably the ones which have an aide-mémoire associated with it, such as actions or an unusual phrasing. It's probably the unfamiliar syntax or vocabulary of the Authorized Version which helps me call to mind verses learned long ago.

The effectual prayer of a righteous man availeth much (James 5:16). I lift up mine eyes unto the hills; from whence cometh mine help? (Psalm 121:1). Go and do thou likewise (Luke 10:37).

I'm not advocating that we return to the language of yesteryear; simply pointing out that the very unfamiliarity makes it more memorable. Although I can't help but feel that if the Authorized Version was good enough for the disciples, it's good enough for me (Ed: what?)

For those of us who are musical – and possibly for those who are not, too – setting scriptures to music (not forcing verses to fit, but writing the music to the rhythm of the verses) gives a natural recollection technique.

Way back in the sixties, a songbook called *Scripture in Song* was published; this contained mostly untouched verses set to music. Usually the songs didn't rhyme, but they scanned well with their tunes, which helps memory.

The charismatic renewal may sometimes be accused of spawning a lot of songs which dumbed-down the truth of the word of God, but there were also lots of excellent songs which were simply scriptures set to music, as I have described. *Sounds of Living Waters* and *Songs of Fellowship*

Volume One were both songbooks with a generous selection of Bible verses with memorable tunes.

The seventies saw *Youth Praise*, with the trail-blazing 12-bar blues version of John 3:16 *Jesus is the Saviour whom I love to know.* Later came *Psalm Praise*, with the fabulous *God is our strength and refuge* set to the rousing theme of *The Dambusters,* (the film about Barnes Wallis, the inventor of the bouncing bomb).

I learned Colossians 1:28 with the help of a lovely tune – these days it's hard to know if the verse reminds me of the tune or if the tune helps me remember the words.

But that doesn't matter much – the truth of 'proclaiming him, admonishing every man with all wisdom, that we may present every man complete in Christ' lives in my head and has a good chance of remaining in my heart.

Maintaining the fun

One of my favourite teaching methods for helping older children and young people remember the words of memory verses is to use accents.

Having a laugh while you're doing something worthwhile doesn't trivialize the importance; rather, it enhances the enjoyment of learning. Using a French or cockney accent can help the phrases to stick in the mind; passing or throwing a ball around a circle puts someone on the spot, which encourages the flow of adrenaline and strengthens memory rather exactingly. Examining doughnuts for outward signs of inward content; creating actions from bad puns; discussing meanings for unusual phrases; all of these help to make the learning process more enjoyable, more interactive and more fun.

Conclusion

Here are 100 ideas for teaching the Bible in a fun way, divided for your convenience into age-appropriate styles. We've included fun ways to teach Bible stories as well as fun ways to teach memory verses, and they are arranged in Bible order within each age group. Many of the teaching methods cn be adapted to teach other verses, or course, but here they are in an appropriate setting. Our hope is that you will feel free to mix and match, and discover new creative ways to keep children's attention on the Word of God.

For even more user-friendliness, one index at the back of the book is arranged in Bible order, and the other is ordered by theme (Love, Jesus, Praise, etc) to help you find resources which serve you as you captivate young hearts and minds with the eternal truth.

Technical Point

Throughout this book, we have used the typographical shorthand of putting words the leader says to the children in **bold print**, and any suggested 'correct' answers to comprehension questions in *italic print* within brackets.

Within each age group section, the listings are given in order of Bible reference, to make them easy to find, and we've tried to indicate general themes and the style or the teaching methods employed. We have also shown which are specifically ways to teach Bible stories, and which are focused on memory verses.

In some cases we have recommended associated songs, all of which appear in the Children's Ministry songbook *250 Songs for Children's Praise & Worship*, along with (in most cases) the name of the album where the song is recorded. These can be obtained (subject to availability) from your local Christian bookshop, online from Children's Ministry at www.childrensministry.co.uk or by phone on 01323 437748.

Working with under 5s

It's never too soon to introduce children to the word of God. In 2 Timothy 3:15 Paul refers to the fact that Timothy was taught the Scriptures 'from infancy'. This was by his mother and grandmother well before the age of five, when his formal scriptural education would have begun.

Our challenge is to make these little ones' first experience of the Bible accessible, understandable, relevant and fun for them. Surely, our desire is that their first encounters with God's word will foster within them an awareness that it is indeed a 'lamp to their feet and a light to their path' (Psalm 119:105) and this will prove true throughout their lives.

But how do we do this?

With under three's, who have a concentration span of about thirty seconds(!) we should always seek to engage their attention first. Relate the Bible story to their experience. For example, with the story of David and Goliath, a few moments comparing sizes of children and adults, and talking about 'big' and 'little' will lead naturally into the story.

With this age it is good to always have a Bible or Bible story book open at the relevant page to reinforce the link between the Bible and the story! The story can then be told using simple language accompanied by actions for the children to join in. Finally, use the last few moments of their attention span to check their understanding with a follow up question such as 'Who was little? Who was big?'

This age group loves repetition (think of the favourite stories they demand to be read to them over and over again!) so the retelling of a very short Bible story – with it's follow up question – will be enjoyed by the children.

As the children reach three years upwards, they are ready to enjoy learning short, relevant Bible verses. Do aim high in your expectations of what can be achieved! I have continually been amazed at the ability of this age group to learn and retain verses. Obviously they won't be able to respond well to the written word, so be inspired by this book and the ideas in the *Children's Ministry Teaching Programme* to be creative in the methods you choose.

Children in this age group, in particular, respond well to music and rhythm, and are able to join in with simple actions and movement. The older the children are, the more they will be interacting with and co-operating with each other, and so will be able to respond well to activities which include the whole group working in unison.

Remember to tie in the memory verse with the Bible theme being taught so that their retention of the verse and their understanding of the teaching are linked together in their minds.

Three's upwards will be able to focus their attention for longer on the telling of a Bible story, but it is important always to include some other activity alongside listening. Try using simple puppets for them to watch or hold up themselves, actions to join in with, or a simple craft to make as they listen.

The children can benefit from participating in an activity which forms part of the story e.g. sharing a 'meal' of bread and fishfingers while listening to the story of the feeding of the five thousand.

This age can be very prone to misunderstandings, so do check their comprehension of the verses and stories being taught. Consider the poor child who thought that Joseph took Mary, Jesus and a flea into Egypt (Matthew 2:13) – whilst a friend's daughter at this age used to sing with great gusto 'My God is so big, so wrong and so mighty'!

These ideas for little ones don't become useless when the children grow older. Equally other ways become appropriate for older children. For example, option 1 of idea 2 is quite suitable for a 9-year-old, as well.

The following suggestions should inspire you – not only to try them out with your children – but also to use the general principles contained within them to create your own ideas.

1

God told Noah to build a boat

Bible Story
Genesis 6:9–22
Theme: Faith
Methods: Actions; music & rhyme

You may reinforce the story by repeating it several times. Encourage children to join in with the actions. Have your own Bible open at Genesis 6:9–22.

Leader says:

God told Noah to build a boat. Put fists together as if hammering.

Build it tall, every wall. Stretch arms up high.

Build it wide and big inside. Stretch arms out wide.

Build it strong, so it lasts long. Flex arms to show muscles.

Build it large. God's in charge! Point up.

God told Noah to build a boat. Put fists together as if hammering.

What did God tell Noah to build?

Teach this song to the children, using the tune *The farmer's in his den.*

God said, 'Build a boat.'	Hammer with fists.
God said, 'Build a boat.'	Hammer with fists.
Noah listened when God spoke.	Put hand to ear.
God said, 'Build a boat.'	Hammer with fists.

2

Memory Verse
Worship the Lord.
Psalm 96:9
Theme: Praise & Worship
Methods: Activity; props; movement; wordplay

Option 1
You will need: Gold material.

Kneel down with everyone in a circle. Have two helpers hold the material over everyone and lift it up high, letting the air underneath, and then letting the cloth settle on the children.

Leader says:

Worship the Lord Bow to the ground

Psalm 96:9 Come back up, and open hands to form a Bible.

Repeat this, with the children and leaders all saying the verse and Bible reference.

Option 2
Children make butterflies from paper, and they hold these up in front of them.

Whisper: **Worship the Lord. Psalm 96:9** Children repeat.
Spoken: **Worship the Lord. Psalm 96:9** Children repeat.
Shout: **Worship the Lord. Psalm 96:9** Children repeat.
Whisper: **We will worship the Lord. Psalm 96:9.**

Children repeat, holding butterfly at waist height.

Spoken: **We will worship the Lord. Psalm 96:9.** Children repeat, holding butterfly at shoulder height.

Shout: **We will worship the Lord. Psalm 96:9.** Children repeat, holding butterfly above head height, and running around to simulate flight.

Remember

We have used the typographical shorthand of putting words the leader says to the children in **bold print**, and any suggested 'correct' answers to comprehension questions in *italic print* within brackets.

Instructions for actions or activities are presented in ordinary type either as part of the script or in a second column, opposite lines of spoken text.

3

Known by God

Bible Story

Psalm 139

Theme: What is God like?

Methods: Actions; music & rhythm

You will need: A Bible.

In advance: Write out the words of the song for helpers, using an overhead projector, white board, flip chart or on paper stuck to the wall.

Encourage children to copy your actions.

Hold up your Bible.

Leader says:

The Bible says that God knows all about us.

God knows when we stand up. Stand up.

God knows when we sit down. Sit down.

God knows when we lie down. Lie down.

God knows when we go here. Stretch an arm one way.

God knows when we go there. Stretch the other arm out.

God knew all about us even before we were born. Make rocking motion with hands.

God knows every day of our lives. Count fingers.

God knows all about me. Point to self.

God knows all about you. Point to others.

Sing this song with your helpers to the tune, *I'm a little teapot*. Repeat, with children marching in place.

God knows all about me. Yes, it's true!
God knows all about me, and you, and you, and you!
God knows when we're happy, grumpy, sad.
He even knows when we are bad!

Associated memory verse:
For all my ways are known to you.
Psalm 119:168.

Have everyone march in place while you say the memory verse aloud. Mime an open book with your hands for the reference. Repeat several times, leaving a gap each time for children to say the missing word. Repeat together, still marching.

4

Memory Verse

A friend loves at all times.

Proverbs 17:17

Themes: Christian life; love

Methods: Movement; wordplay

Option 1

Leader says: **Sometimes we need friends to help us learn about Jesus. Can you say our Bible words after me? A friend loves at all times.** Children repeat.

Proverbs 17:17. Children repeat. Show the verse in the Bible.

Proverbs is the name of the book where we find these words.

Divide the children into two groups, each with a helper. One group says the verse and the other says the reference. Then they swap over. Repeat until the children can say the verse and the reference.

Option 2

Demonstrate these actions with a helper. Hold hands and swing arms, repeating the memory verse and reference together. Repeat with children several times.

5

Jesus is born

Bible Story (particularly useful for under 3s)

Luke 2:1–7

Theme: Jesus

Methods: Actions; activity

You will need: Sheets of paper; self-adhesive farm animal stickers; masking tape.

In advance: Tape the sheets of paper to the table, to stop them slipping, using masking tape at each corner.

You may reinforce the story by repeating it several times. Encourage children to join in with the actions. Have your own Bible or a story Bible open at Luke 2:1–7.

Leader says: **Mary and Joseph went to Bethlehem.** Walk feet on the spot.

The only place to stay was in a stable. Rest your head on your hands.

In the stable, Jesus was born. Pretend to rock a baby.

Mary wrapped up her baby, Jesus, to keep him warm. Continue rocking.

Baby Jesus slept in the stable, with the animals around. Rest your head on your hands.

Jesus was born!

Where was Jesus born? *(Accept on-topic answers)*

Encourage children to stick animal stickers on their paper. Talk about the animals that would have been in the stable that Mary, Joseph and Jesus stayed in.

6

Jesus heals ten lepers

Bible Story

Luke 17:11–19

Theme: Jesus

Methods: Actions; props

You will need: Strips of cloth or bandages.

In advance: Tie a bandage round your knee.

Say the rhyme, showing the bandage.

Leader says:

When I fall down and graze my knee,
It's as sore as it can be.
Let's pretend you've hurt your knee,
And put a bandage on, like me.

Have helpers tie bandages on children's knees. Every time TEN men are mentioned, hold up TEN fingers for children to copy. Leader says:

Long ago, when Jesus lived, there were TEN men who
had some sore places.

They had sore knees.	Pat knees.
They had sore toes.	Wiggle toes.
They had sore fingers.	Wiggle fingers.
They had sore noses.	Rub nose.

No one wanted to be near the TEN men. Everyone was
afraid they might get sores, too, if they came too

close. People told the TEN men to go away. The TEN men were sad.

One day, Jesus saw the TEN men. They called out, 'Jesus, please help us!' Jesus cared about the TEN men. Jesus sent the TEN men to find the priest. The priest was like a church leader. If he said the TEN men were better, they could go home again to their families.

As the TEN men went to find the priest, they saw that their skin was better (leader removes her bandage).

The sore places had gone! The TEN men were so excited and ran to the priest. But one man came back (hold up one finger).

He knelt down in front of Jesus (kneel down).

'You made my sore places better! Thank you! Thank you!' He was the only one who came back to say thank you to Jesus.

Help children remove their bandages, saying, 'I'm better! I'm better! Thank you, Jesus!'

Associated memory verse:
We give thanks to you, Lord God.
Revelation 11:17.
Make a kneeling circle and hold up TEN fingers. Count off each finger as you say the verse and reference. Repeat until learned.
Leader says:
Jesus is so good to us. We can always say thank you to him.

7

Memory Verse

Jesus said, 'If you love me, you will obey what I command.'

John 14:15

Themes: Christian Life; Jesus

Methods: Activity; movement

You will need: A ball.

Sit in a circle, with the children facing inwards, legs out-stretched. In turn, roll the ball to helper, saying the words of the memory verse and the reference. They roll the ball back to you, repeating the words (and reference). Then repeat with each of the children, helping them as necessary. Leader says:

Jesus wants us to love and obey him.

8

Jesus is alive!
Bible Story (specially suitable for under-3s)
John 20:1–18.
Theme: Jesus
Method: Actions

Here is a way of telling the difficult story of Christ's death and resurrection to under-threes. The language and ideas used are carefully chosen to be suitable for this age group.

Encourage the children to join in with the actions.

Leader says:
Some people didn't like Jesus. Shake head, no.
They hurt Jesus, and took him away. His friends were sad. Sad face.
They thought Jesus would never come back. Shake head, no. Show surprise.
Then Mary saw Jesus alive and well! Nod head, yes.
She told Jesus' friends, 'Jesus is alive!' Happy face.
Jesus' friends were happy again. Clap hands.
Jesus is alive!
Who is alive? All join in, shouting 'Jesus is alive!'

9

Jesus makes breakfast for his friends

Bible Story

John 21:1–14

Theme: Jesus

Method: Activity; props

This Bible story can be used as an outdoor activity, with a pretend barbecue, time and place permitting.

You will need: Masking tape; scissors; large piece of garden netting or muslin; helper dressed as Jesus; stones; red crepe paper; grill grid; fish shaped nuggets and bread or tuna sandwiches cut with a fish shaped cutter.

In advance: Mark out a boat shape on the floor with the masking tape, or create a boat shape outdoors. Check for any food allergies.

Have a helper prepare the pretend fire while you tell the story. One leader will need to speak the words of Jesus.

Leader says: **One night, Jesus' friends went fishing. Let's join them.** Sit everyone in the boat. **They fished with a big net.** Have everyone hold the net. **They kept hold of it, and let it down into the water.** Let the net over the side of the boat. **When they pulled the net up, there were no fish flapping in it.** Pull the net in.

   Then they let the net down into the water on the other side of the boat. Repeat the action and words.

They did it again on the other side. Repeat the action and words. **Jesus' friends fished all night, and didn't catch one fish! They were tired and hungry and decided to go home. Someone called out from the beach:**

Jesus: Have you caught any fish?

Leader: **What did they say?** *(No, we haven't.)*

Jesus: Let down the net again, and you'll find some.

Leader: **Jesus' friends trusted the man and did as they were told.** Lower the net. **Suddenly, the net was full of flapping fish! The man on the beach was their friend Jesus! No one else could catch fish for them! Jesus made a barbecue breakfast for everyone.** Take children to sit around the pretend fire.

Jesus: Come and have breakfast.

Leader: **So they did! Jesus always cares for his friends. They were glad they had trusted Jesus.** Share out the bread and fish or tuna sandwiches with everyone.

Associated memory verse:

He cares for those who trust in him. Nahum 1:7.

You will need: Paper; wax crayons; scissors; netting from Bible story.

In advance: Tear or cut different sized fish shapes from paper.

Children can scribble-colour the fish shapes and place them in the net. Have everyone hold the net and gently shake it up and down. Adults can repeat the verse and reference together several times, encouraging children to join in.

10

Memory Verse

Jesus went around doing good.

Acts 10:38

Theme: Jesus; Prayer

Method: Music; movement

Option 1

You will need: Open Bible

Leader says: **One of the good things Jesus did was to tell us how to talk to God.**

Action: March everyone around the room following you, while you repeat the verse and reference.

Option 2

Join hands in a circle. Sing this song to the tune *Oh Dear, what can the matter be?* All sing

Je-sus went around doing good. Circle left.

Je-sus went around doing good. Circle right.

Je-sus went around doing good. Circle left.

He is so good to me.   Step towards centre,
                                  swinging hands upwards.

Associated songs:

Jesus' hands were kind hands

124 in *250 Songs for Children's Praise & Worship*

11

Philip talks about Jesus

Bible Story

Acts 8:1–8

Theme: Salvation

Methods: Puppets; music & rhythm

You will need: Thin card; scissors; wax crayons; glue sticks; craft sticks; xylophone and striker.

In advance: draw and colour a simple shape of a man with an outline around him. Cut out the outline and supply one per child. Help children draw, colour, and cut out the figure, and then glue it to a craft stick or similar.

Hold up your puppet.

Leader says:

This is a man called Philip. Say his name with me. Children repeat the name. Have a helper play two notes on a xylophone, one for each syllable of his name.

Sing Philip's name to the two notes. Each time Philip's name is mentioned, have the same two notes played. **Each time I say, 'Philip' you can hold him up and sing his name with me.**

Philip (Philip) **went to a new place. Philip** (Philip) **talked about Jesus. Philip** (Philip) **talked about how much Jesus loves us. Philip** (Philip) **told about the wonderful things Jesus did.**

People listened when Philip (Philip) **talked about**

Jesus. Poorly people were made well as Philip (Philip) **talked about Jesus.**

People were very glad Philip (Philip) **talked about Jesus.**

Associated memory verse:

I will tell of all your wonders. Psalm 9:1.

Have your helper rhythmically beat two notes on the xylophone in sequence while you sing the words aloud. Repeat several times, with children clapping or joining in the words.

Remember

We have used the typographical shorthand of putting words the leader says to the children in **bold print**, and any suggested 'correct' answers to comprehension questions in *italic print* within brackets.

Instructions for actions or activities are presented in ordinary type either as part of the script or in a second column, opposite lines of spoken text.

12

Memory Verse
God sent his Son.
Galatians 4:4
Theme: Salvation
Methods: Music; props
You will need: Red and green stickers.

Divide children into pairs, facing each other. They can hold hands and swing them to the rhythm of the words of the verse. Give one child of each pair a red sticker, and the other a green sticker. They should stick these on their hands.

Green sticker children say: God sent his Son.

Red sticker children say: Galatians 4:4

Repeat several times until the rhythm is established; then swap over.

Leader says: **We are sharing the good news, just like the shepherds did. God's Son is born! Can you say these words with me and do the actions? God sent his Son.** Point up. **For all the world to see.** Make binoculars with hands. **We shout out loud and cheer for God.** Shout and cheer. **And praise him joyfully.** Stretch arms high and wide.

Repeat several times, encouraging the children to do the actions as they say the words aloud.

13

Memory Verse

Always try to be kind to each other.

1 Thessalonians 5:15

Theme: Christian life

Methods: Activity; music; wordplay

Option 1

Stand children in two rows, facing each other. Leader says: **Always try to be kind to each other**. Children in first row repeat. Leader says: **1 Thessalonians 5:15.** Children in second row repeat; holding open Bibles (or miming).

Repeat a few times, then change the order, so that the row which was previously assigned to the reference becomes the row saying the verse, and vice versa.

Option 2

You will need: A ball of string.

Make a circle of chairs, facing outward. Children can kneel on them, facing inwards.

Tie the string to one chair back and ask that child to repeat the word 'Always'. Cross the circle and thread the string through another chair back, asking that child to repeat 'try'. Begin to weave a web of string, criss-crossing the circle and asking children to repeat the words of the verse (and the reference) as their chair is included in the web.

Continue several times through the verse, until you run out of string.

Option 3

Gather children into several groups of three of more. Groups say the words of the verse and the reference in turn: i.e. group one starts with 'Always'; group 2 says 'try'; group 3 says 'to' etc. Continue several times through the memory verse. Start in a new place each time to ensure each group has to know different words!

Option 4

Sit with the children in a circle and show them how to pat knees and clap hands alternately to a slow rhythm. Use these actions to the rhythm of the words of the memory verse, saying the words out loud. Practise until everyone can join in.

14

Memory verse

He cares for you.

1 Peter 5:7

Theme: Love

Method: Actions; music; movement; wordplay

Option 1

Clap in rhythm, saying the words and the reference. Repeat with children several times.

Option 2

Whisper the words of the memory verse and the reference around a circle of children, passing the message on. Then introduce a tablespoon, and show the children how they can see their reflection in the spoon. As each child receives the spoon as it is passed around, they should declare to themselves, 'He cares for you. 1 Peter 5:7.'

Option 3

You will need: Several pairs of shoes, boots, sandals. Leader says: **Jesus cares for us and wants us to follow him.** Have children wear shoes on hands as well as feet, or remove their own shoes and wear them on their hands. Demonstrate how to crawl forward, one foot or hand at a time, as you say each word of the memory verse and the reference. Repeat several times.

Option 4

Show children how to pretend to row a boat, and then repeat the words of the memory verse and the reference in time to the rowing action.

15

Memory Verse

God is love.

1 John 4:8

Theme: Love

Methods: Action; activity; movement; music; props

Option 1

You will need: Coloured paper; sticky tape; scissors; a Bible.

In advance: Make a paper crown and a heart shape for everyone.

Give out crowns and heart shapes. Stand some distance away from a Bible in the centre of a circle.

Leader says:	**God is**
Action:	Hold up crown.
Leader says:	**Love**
Action:	Hold heart shape to chest.
Leader says:	**1 John 4:8**
Action:	Run to Bible.

Option 2

You will need: Rhythm instruments.

Demonstrate how to use the instruments with the words and the rhythm. Encourage children to join in. Let each child have a turn to say the words and the reference while everyone else plays.

Working with Fives to Nines

This age group in general is very active – they love running about and making a lot of noise! In my own church it is no coincidence that it is this group who have been allocated the sports hall in which to meet!

Use this energy to your advantage through the methods you use to teach both memory verses and Bible stories. Their physical co-ordination is fast developing, opening up the possibilities of physical activities. They can play hop-scotch on the words of a verse; or games such as all standing in a circle and throwing a soft ball to one another – who-ever catches the ball says the memory verse, or one word of it.

Fives to nines also respond well to music and rhythm so whether they are clapping out rhythms, enjoying the challenge of 'rapping' a verse, or fitting words to their favourite tunes, these methods will help fix Scripture into their minds and hearts.

This age group is much better at interacting with one

another so whole group activities should work well. For example, idea 34 'Great is our Lord and mighty in power' (Psalm 147:5) will involve the whole group working together – and also using up some energy!

The children will still not necessarily be fluent in their reading and writing skills so don't put too much emphasis on these. It's important not to embarrass strugglers in front of their peers and thus run the risk of putting them off the word of God by our insensitivity. On the other hand, some children love reading and excel at it and should be given the opportunity to do so.

When teaching Bible stories to this age group, we find that the children can cope with longer, more complex stories and methods of learning, but will always need to have their attention engaged by more than just listening.

Their ability to participate in role play is developing, and this opens up even greater opportunities for them to interact and become part of the story themselves. For instance Acts 25: 23-27, when Paul is on trial before King Agrippa. The children can take the part of the soldiers, marching in time, bringing Paul – played by a helper – to the King. In the *Children's Ministry Teaching Programme*, stories such as these are provided already recorded on the resource CD so the children can march in time as they listen to, and act out the story.

Another fun method is for the children and helpers to make an environment appropriate for the telling of the story. You could make a tent out of chairs and old sheets that the children can sit in while hearing about Paul's trade as a tent maker. Or create a boat shape from chairs that they can get into and pretend to row as they hear about the storm on Lake Galilee and Jesus walking on the water – they will also enjoy making the appropriate 'weather' noises to accompany the storm!

Again, there is still a place for simple reading and writing activities – or maybe drawing appropriate parts of the story, so long as leaders are sensitive to individual abilities – this works much better as a small group activity rather than the children working on their own. *Children's Ministry Teaching Programme* uses this method to great effect in the activity sheets KidZone Blue and KidZone Gold and has the advantage of giving the children a tangible record of the story for them to keep.

As with the under-fives, it is imperative to keep checking for evidence of understanding of the Bible story. They should never be taught in isolation but always following an introduction relating to their own experiences – then succeeded by activities which allow them to explore the content and concepts in the teaching; concluding with a challenge about the importance of this in their own lives.

Finally, remember that all children develop at different speeds. So be flexible – it may well be that some of the activities in this book suggested for under-fives will work well with children aged six or even seven, whilst the over-nines' activities could prove to be suitable for your younger children as well.

16

Adam & Eve disobey God
Bible Story
Genesis 3:1–24
Theme: What is God like?
Method: Activity

Invite the young people to draw serpents and to give them colourful skins with pretty patterns. As they draw and colour in, explain that although the serpent looked very nice, he was evil and tempted Eve and Adam to disobey God. Not everything that looks good is good.

Associated memory verse:
For all have sinned and fall short of the glory of God.
Romans 3:23
Make a slow, rhythmic snake-like conga around your meeting space and repeat the words of the verse and reference together.

17

Noah loved God

Bible Story

Genesis 6:5–21

Theme: Christian Life

Method: Drama

You will need: Adults to mime God and Noah; card crown; stage block.

God stands on the stage block, wearing the crown. Everyone else stands very still in front of God. Noah does not join in the people's disobedience.

Children can follow your instructions as the Bible story progresses. Repeat the story and mime to benefit from the continuity.

God gave people the gift of life. God holds out his hands and blows.

People took his gift of life. People move and stretch.

God gave people the gift of love. God throws his crown into the crowd.

God wanted people to love him, too. God reaches out his hands to the people.

People took his gift of love, and trampled it into pieces. People stamp on crown.

People turned away from God. People turn their backs on God.

And lived their lives without him. People take four paces forward.

God looked to see if there was anyone who loved him. God looks out.

Of all the people on the earth, only Noah loved God. Noah reaches out to God.

Noah worshipped God. Noah kneels down.

Noah talked to God. Noah lifts his hands in prayer.

Noah listened to God. Noah lifts his head, listening.

God was upset that people wouldn't love him. God puts his head in his hands.

God was angry that people were so wicked. God shakes his head.

God said he would clean the earth of such wickedness. God sweeps his hands in front of him.

God said he would start again with Noah and his family. God points to Noah. Everyone else sits down. Noah approaches God.

God shared his plans with Noah and gave him exact instructions. God and Noah measure with hands.

God told Noah to build an ark to keep his family and animals from every species safe. God was going to flood the whole earth and make it clean to start again.

Associated memory verse:
Show me your ways, O Lord, teach me your paths. Psalm 25:4
See idea 27.

18

Lot learns about obedience

Bible Story

Genesis 13:1—14:16

Theme: Christian Life

Method: Activity

Here are some activities which help emphasize the theme of how we can be influenced by others; positively or negatively. Our goal is to obey God. In the story of Abraham and Lot, we see Lot being influenced negatively by the people among whom he chooses to live.

Option 1

In advance: Brief the adult helpers to give agreed wrong answers to the questions.

Select several older children and one or two adults to line up facing the others. Ask the following questions to each of the lines in turn, starting with the adults. Take care not to give the right answers until all the questions have been asked.

1 **Add 27 and 21.**

Adults answer: 49. Correct answer: 48.

2 **What colour do you get if you mix red and blue paints?**

Adults answer: brown. Correct answer: purple.

3 How many legs does a spider have?
Adults answer: six. Correct answer: eight.

4 How do you spell teeth?
Adults answer: T-E-E-F. Correct answer: T-E-E-T-H.

5 What is a 'teepee'?
Adults answer: a chinese teapot. Correct answer: a Native American tent.

6 Who writes the books about Harry Potter?
Adults answer: J A Rowling. Correct answer: J K Rowling.

Perhaps some children will have been influenced into agreeing with the wrong answers, because they expected the adults to be giving right answers. Even if you have super-confident children who knew they were right despite the influence of the adults, explain that some people are more easily swayed away from the truth.

Then tell the story of Abraham and Lot, emphasising that Lot was unhelpfully influenced by the people all around him. We can make the same mistake.

Option 2
You will need: Table, chalk or masking tape, table tennis ball.
In advance: Mark a line down the centre of a table with chalk or masking tape, longways.

Create two teams, on opposite sides of the table. Place the ball on the centre line, in the middle of the table. Upon the command *1-2-3-Go!* both teams must blow, attempting to make the ball fall off the opposite edge of the table. No-one may use their hands or lean over the table. If the ball falls off the side, the referee must return it to the centre line. Keep score, and give a prize to the winning team, who may need a while to recover their puff!

Conclude by pointing out that one team influenced the ball one way, while the other team tried to influence it the opposite way. Sometimes, this can be like our friends; we may want to be like them, but they may influence us into doing something we know is wrong.

We want to allow God to influence us to do the right things.

Option 3
You can count on it.
Here is a poem by Ruth Alliston about things we *can* rely upon. Read it slowly, and invite children to brainstorm ideas for suitable actions. Once these are agreed (or you agree that everyone can do their own thing), read it again.

> Someone's first, someone's last;
> Bubbles burst, bombs blast.
> Raindrops fall, puddles splash;
> Snakes crawl, plates smash.
> Thunder rumbles, hunger nibbles;
> A child tumbles, baby dribbles.
> Pain brings tears, love mends;
> Hugs help fears, night-time ends.

Remind everyone that we can count on all these things, and we can rely on God being faithful and true, as well.

Option 4
Friends stick together and rely on each other.
You will need: Old, clean tights or similar; chalk or masking tape.
Match children of even size, and tie them together for three-legged races. Create a start and finish line with chalk or masking tape. If you have room, everyone can race together, but if not, you'll need heats with winners and runners-up proceeding to the next round and then to the final.
Leader says: **Remember, good friends stick together, help each other, try not to become impatient with each other, have a laugh together, want what's best for each other, and share the prize.**

Associated memory verse:
Teach me to do your will, for you are my God.
Psalm 143:10
Invite children to take turns to pretend to be the teacher, while others play the part of the pupils. Say the words and reference aloud several times, explaining how we can know God's will, and why we need to know God's will. Continue to repeat until all can say the verse with confidence.

19

Miriam takes care of Moses

Bible Story for younger children

Exodus 2:1–10

Theme: Love

Method: Activity

You will need: Paper; green crayons; scissors; blue material; reusable adhesive putty; basket; doll; blanket; table.

In advance: Cut or tear long paper strips approximately 8cms wide.

Children can scribble colour the paper strips with green crayons. Leader says: **Miriam was very excited. She had a new baby brother. His name was Moses.**

Miriam's mummy and daddy loved baby Moses and Miriam helped them take care of him. But the king was not pleased. The king said, 'There are too many boy babies.'

The king sent his soldiers to hurt the little boys. Moses' mummy put Moses in a special basket which floated. Place the doll in the basket with the blanket.

Moses' mummy took the basket to the river. Lay the blue material in ripples under the table.

Moses' mummy floated the basket at the edge of the water. Place the basket on the material under the table.

There were lots of green reeds growing at the edge of the water. The green reeds (some people call them

'bulrushes') hid the basket. Help children fix their 'reeds' to the top edge of the table.

Miriam stayed near her baby brother to make sure he was safe. Place finger on lips.

The king's daughter, the princess, came to the river. Hold a pretend crown on your head.

She saw the basket in the green reeds and picked it up. Part the reeds and pick up the basket.

Baby Moses was crying. Take out the doll and rock it. Pass the doll around for children to hold.

The princess said she would take the baby home and look after him. Miriam asked the princess if she needed someone to help her take care of the baby. The princess said she did. Miriam ran home to find her mummy. Miriam had looked after her baby brother well, and he was kept safe from the king and his soldiers.

Miriam's mummy looked after baby Moses until he was old enough to become part of the royal family. God had kept baby Moses safe, because God had plans for Moses to lead his people.

20

Through the Red Sea

Bible Story

Exodus 13:17—15:21

Theme: Salvation

Methods: Music; props

You will need: Teddy Bear; a large piece of red material; small drum or bongo; a large stone (for safety's sake, and for demonstration) too big to swallow.

Show the teddy bear and explain that soft toys are cuddly and safe, even though real bears are big and dangerous. They have large claws and can be very angry when disturbed.

Leader says: **If you were being chased by a large black bear, you would be very frightened, I expect. The bear could do some damage to you, which would be scary. How does it feel to be afraid?** Accept on-topic answers, and then show children how to find their pulse on their wrist.

The pulse shows that our hearts are pumping and that the blood is flowing. That's a good thing, and quite normal! When we are afraid, our hearts beat faster. Beat the drum to demonstrate.

We might feel like we're being smothered, and we can't breathe. Cover yourself with the red material.

Or we might feel like we can't swallow, with a big lump in our throats. Show the stone. Pass around the material and stone.

What makes you afraid? *(Accept answers.)*

What can you do when you're afraid? *(Accept answers.)*

God saved the Israelites from danger. Some of them were afraid, but God saved them.

Using Exodus 13:17—15:21, retell the story in a dramatic way. When the Israelites see the Egyptian Army coming, cover the children with the red material. When God opens the Red sea to allow the Israelites to walk across on dry land, remove the material.

Associated memory verse:

With God, nothing is impossible.

Luke 1:37

In advance: Write out each of the words and reference on separate pieces of paper.

Fix words randomly to the red material; children can sort them out into the right order. Holding the stone as a pointer, in turn, they can read the verse aloud. Leader says:

We can trust God to help us, just as he helped the Israelites get away from their enemies.

21

Memory Verse for older children

You shall have no other gods before me. You shall not make for yourself an idol. You shall not misuse the name of the Lord your God.

Exodus 20:3–4,7

Theme: Christian Life

Method: Activity

You will need: Paper; felt pens; Bibles.

Make small groups, each with a helper. Children can find the memory verse and make a group or individual poster to show its meaning.

Associated song:

Worship No God

242 in *250 Songs for Children's Praise and Worship*

Recorded on *12 New Children's Praise Songs Vol 1* CHMCD001

22

Hannah rejoices

Bible story

1 Samuel 1:1—2:21

Theme: Praise and worship

Method: Props

You will need: Paper tissues, mirror, calendar, shawl or babygro, paper heart, various sizes of children's clothes.

Place all these items in a box, and invite children to step forward to find the various items as you tell the story.

Hannah was upset because she had no child.   Paper tissues.

Eli the priest said God had heard her prayer and would give her what she asked. Pass round the mirror for everyone to smile at their reflection.

Hannah still had to wait. Calendar.

At last, little baby Samuel was born. Shawl or babygro.

When Samuel was a little boy, Hannah took him to the temple to serve God. Paper heart; hug each other.

Each year, Hannah took new clothes for Samuel, as he grew bigger. Assorted clothes.

God heard and answered Hannah's prayer, and she was thankful.

Associated memory verse:

Be glad and rejoice. Surely the Lord has done great things.

Joel 2:21

You will need: Balloons, double sheet or play parachute.

In advance: Blow up the balloons and store in a bin liner or similar.

Invite the children to stand around the edges of the sheet or parachute, holding it at waist height. Release the balloons onto the sheet. Show children how to step in to the circle and back out, tensioning the sheet, causing the balloons to be tossed into the air.

Shout the words of the memory verse as you do this. Have fun!

Remember

We have used the typographical shorthand of putting words the leader says to the children in **bold print**, and any suggested 'correct' answers to comprehension questions in *italic print* within brackets.

Instructions for actions or activities are presented in ordinary type either as part of the script or in a second column, opposite lines of spoken text.

23

God's way is best

Bible Story

1 Samuel 8:1—10:26

Theme: Christian Life

Method: Drama

Option 1

Second best for Amanda

You will need: Helper to play the part of Amanda, dressed in school uniform. This will entertain the children; even more so if the helper is male! Having broken the ice, interview Amanda in this way:

Let's welcome Amanda. She's come to visit us today. You look a bit down in the dumps, Amanda!

A *(sighing)* I did something really stupid.

Oh dear. What did you do?

A *(silence)*

Do you want to tell us about it?

A Not really.

OK. We all do stupid things sometimes.

A I'm in the school choir, you see. The music teachers say I've got a good voice, and I really enjoy singing. Anyway, they were planning a concert tour in America. They said there would be lots of extra rehearsals after school and that we would have to save up to pay for the trip. But we

could make up our own minds about whether we wanted
to go.

What an opportunity, Amanda!

A Yeah. But none of my friends were in the choir, and all
the extra practices sounded like a lot of work. And I
haven't got all that much money, and I didn't want to
save up… So I said no, I won't go. I was put in another
choir, for the end of term concert, but it wasn't the
same so I gave that up, too.

**Oh dear. Well, I suppose you made your mind up.
Why the long face?**

A When the others went off to America, they were so
excited. I wanted to go with them, but of course I
couldn't. I was jealous. I hear they are having a great
time.

**Sounds like hard work, though. But a marvellous
experience!**

A Yeah. But my parents were cross. The music teachers
were cross with me. I got fed up and I've fallen out with
my friends because they think I'm miserable and they
are right! I made the wrong choice. It's so hard to know
what is the right thing to do.

Consider with the children:

**What would have happened if Amanda had chosen to
go with the choir?** (*Hard work learning the songs; lots of prac-
tising; saving up; making new friends in the choir; going to America.*)

What happened because she chose not to go? (*Upset her*

parents and the music teachers; felt left out when the choir went off; didn't enjoy singing with the other choir; became miserable and fell out with her friends.)

Do you think she could have guessed what might happen? How could she have helped herself make a good decision? Sometimes we just can't tell what is the best thing to do. Where can we get help with this sort of decision? *(Parents; older friends; the Bible; people at church; through prayer.)*

Turn to 1 Samuel 16:1–13, summarising the story of how God helped Samuel to choose David to be the next king.

Option 2
Treasure Hunt
You will need: Newspaper, cardboard boxes, some small containers, sequins or small beads (from craft shops); a die and shaker.

Invite children to help you shred the newspaper and fill three or four cardboard boxes. They should wash their hands afterwards. Then add a handful of beads or sequins to each box, shaking them down among the shredded newspaper.

Divide the children into as many teams as you have cardboard boxes, and line them up as far from the boxes as possible. A leader shakes the die, and when a six is shaken out, the first person in each team is to rush to their cardboard box and begin to fill their container with beads or sequins. They continue, and the leader continues, until another six is thrown, when the next person in each team goes to the cardboard box, takes the container from the first child and continues to hunt for beads or sequins. If throwing a six proves too elusive, change the rules as you go along and allow any number over three to cause a change of player, so that everyone gets a turn before all the beads or sequins are found.

Conclude by pointing out that God knows us on the inside, and can see past the rubbish. He knows that there's treasure hidden inside, just as he did when he recognized the value in David.

Associated memory verse:
I will listen to what God the Lord will say.
Psalm 85:8.

Option 1
Say the verse aloud while another leader reads from a newspaper. Ask the children to listen carefully only to you, and read the verse again, while two or three helpers read aloud different passages from different newspapers or magazines. Then see if any of the children have been able to work out what you were saying.

Explain that they need to listen carefully, and not be distracted. In the same way, we need to listen carefully to what God says. Continue without the distractions until all have learned the verse and reference.

Option 2

Invite the children to kneel in a circle, facing inwards. Say the verse and reference together three or four times, and then say one word each, proceeding around the circle, standing when it is your turn to say the next word, creating a Mexican wave.

24

David & Goliath

Bible Story

1 Samuel 17:1–54

Theme: Salvation

Method: Props

Summarize the Bible story, using the present tense, lots of pictorial language and an exciting tone.

Ask the children to consider what things in life seem to be too large to deal with easily, like when they are frightened of things or face big disappointments. Sometimes grown-ups might let them down, or there might be other children at school who act in a way which is unpleasant or unkind. Allow children to suggest 'giants', valuing what they say, and not planting suggestions of things which you think they should be scared about. Conclude with an opportunity to pray together.

Give each child a small pebble, and ask them to think of a place at home where they can keep it (for example, on their bedside table, near the bathroom mirror, in their pyjama pocket). It should be a place where they will notice the pebble several times a day or especially when they get ready for bed. Tell them that the pebble is to remind them that God will help them face 'giants' in their life.

Prayer: Father God, with a pebble like this you helped David defeat the giant Goliath, who was making your people afraid. We don't want to be afraid of the giants we face. Help us to be brave and bold and strong and to trust you for your help. Amen.

Associated Memory Verse:

Be strong in the Lord and in his mighty power. Ephesians 6:10

You will need: Thick elastic bands, newspaper, a target.

In advance: Draw a target onto a piece of A3 paper. Concentric circles would be good; the shape of a man's head would be ideal. Also write the words and reference of the memory verse on this piece of paper. With reusable self-adhesive putty, position the target at a height of about three metres off the ground, representing Goliath's head. Practice using the elastic bands as a sling, using scrunched-up balls of newspaper as ammo.

Show children how to use the elastic bands as slings, warning that you will remove slings from anyone using them against another child or adult. In turn, children can read the verse and reference aloud and then take three shots at the target.

God is always able to hit the target of giants in our lives.

Associated song:

Goliath Thump Thump

68 in *250 Songs for Children's Praise and Worship*

Recorded on *New Songs 94/95 Vol 1* SFCD293

25

Bible Story

Nehemiah and his friends build the city wall

Nehemiah 4

Theme: Christian Life

Method: Props; activity

You will need: Interlocking bricks – Lego, Duplo or similar.

Make several circles of children and helpers, each with a pile of bricks.

Leader says: **In Bible times, people built big, strong walls around their towns and cities. The big, strong walls kept bad people out. People felt safe inside their towns and cities.**

There had been a big, strong wall around the city of Jerusalem, but bad people knocked the wall down. Nehemiah loved God. Nehemiah knew God wanted a big, strong wall around Jerusalem. Nehemiah and his friends started to build the wall again. They worked hard and joined all the bricks together. Helpers and children can begin to join bricks together.

The bad people came back and shouted nasty things at the builders. They didn't want Nehemiah and his friends to build a big, strong wall around Jerusalem. The bad people said, 'Stop building that wall, or we'll hurt you!'

Nehemiah told his friends not to be frightened of the bad people. God cared that they were frightened. God would help them to be brave. God did help them to be brave, and they finished building the wall. It was a big, strong wall again all around Jerusalem. Help children join the different parts of the wall together.

God cares when we're frightened, too.

26

Memory Verse

May the words of my mouth and the meditation of my heart be pleasing in your sight, O Lord.

Psalm 19:14

Theme: Christian Life; Prayer

Methods: Action; activity; props

You will need: Red paper; pens; scissors; sticks of glue; craft sticks.

In advance: Write out the memory verse.

Children can draw and cut out lips and a heart shape each, to stick onto craft sticks. Using hearts and lips, children can make up actions for the memory verse. Read the memory verse together several times.

Leader says: **Meditation is thinking slowly and carefully. God knows what is in our hearts when we pray to him, or speak to others. He is pleased when what we say matches what is in our hearts.**

27

Memory Verse

Show me your ways, O Lord, teach me your paths.

Psalms 25:4

Theme: Christian Life

Method: Movement

In advance: Line and space some chairs like a slalom.

Children line up at the start and say the Bible verse twice. They can make their way through the slalom, and back again, repeating the verse and reference.

Associated song:

Lord, tell me your ways

145 in *250 Songs for Children's Praise and Worship*

Recorded on *Wakey Wakey Sleepy Sleepy* KMCD958

28

Memory Verse

Wait for the Lord; be strong and take heart and wait for the Lord.
Psalm 27:14
Theme: Christian Life
Method: Action

Ask the children to estimate 15 seconds. Some will find it almost impossible to be quiet for this length of time!
Leader says: **It's hard to wait even a little while, sometimes. The Bible teaches us to wait for the Lord. We can be sure that he will keep his promise.**

Learn the verse by dramatising the word 'wait' each time it occurs by leaving a pause (sometimes long, sometimes even longer), and by using actions for 'strong' (muscle man pose) and 'take heart' (mime removing a beating heart from your chest).

Psalm 27:14. (pause) **Wait for the Lord; be strong and take heart and** (pause) **wait for the Lord. Psalm 27:14.**

29

Exploring Psalms

Bible Teaching

Themes: Praise & Worship; Prayer

Methods: Music & rhythm

You will need: Bibles; musical and rhythm instruments.

In advance: Make six signs:

• Praise • Help • Forgiveness • Thanks • Trust • Power.

Alternatively, as an additional activity, children can make their own signs or banners, and decorate them.

Help children find the book of Psalms in their Bibles. Leader says: **Psalms are poems, songs and prayers written by people long ago who loved God. Some Psalms were written by David, the singing, soldier king.**

Some psalms praise God for his love and kindness. Some psalms are about how God helps us. Some psalms ask for God's forgiveness. Some psalms thank God for his care. Some psalms tell how God can be trusted. Some psalms show God's great power.

Show the six signs. Read the following verses from Psalms. Help children decide to which category each verse belongs. Using instruments, voices and bodies, help children explore, decide and practise appropriate sounds and rhythm for each category. Repeat the verses. Have a helper hold up the sign for each verse. Children can accompany it with their chosen sounds and rhythms.

• **Praise**

I will praise you, God, with all my heart. I will sing your praise. I will bow down towards your worship house. I praise you for your love. I praise you for keeping your promises. (Psalm 138:1–2)

• **Help**

God is like a safe place to be. He is strong. He is our helper when there is trouble. (Psalm 46:1)

• **Forgiveness**

Be kind to me, God. Show me your love that never stops. Erase my sin because you are so kind. Wash away all my sin and clean my heart. (Psalm 51:1–2)

• **Thanks**

I will thank God with all my heart. I will praise him with people who do what is right. (Psalm 111:1)

• **Trust**

I trust God. He saves me. He is like a fortress. Nothing can shake me. I am safe with him. (Psalm 62:1–2)

• **Power**

God is King! Greatness is like a robe he wears. He is strong. The world stays where God put it. It cannot be moved. (Psalm 93:1–2)

30

Memory Verse

God is our refuge and strength, an ever-present help in trouble

Psalm 46:1

Theme: Faith

Methods: Action; wordplay

Make a circle. Say the verse and reference twice, slowly.

Leader says:

What is a refuge? *(Somewhere safe.)*

What does ever-present mean? *(Always with us.)*

Repeat the verse slowly with actions.

Leader says:	**God is our refuge**
Action:	Make a tower shape with hands over head
Leader says:	**and strength;**
Action:	Raise hands making fists.
Leader says:	**an ever-present help in trouble.**
Action:	Arms around each other's shoulders
Leader says:	**Psalm 46:1.**
Action:	Open hands like a Bible.

Repeat several times.

31

Memory Verse

As for me, I will trust in you.

Psalm 55:23

Theme: Christian Life

Method: Movement

You will need: Chalk or masking tape.

Mark a start line and stand everyone along it. Take steps forward, repeating the memory verse and reference aloud. Return to the start line and repeat the steps with the child next to you. Continue adding one more child each time until everyone is included.

If you have a large group, this could take nearly for ever, so perhaps leaders could work in unison and each take an additional child with them each time.

32

Memory Verse

Your word, O Lord, is eternal
Psalm 119:89

Theme: Christian Life
Methods: Movement; wordplay

Option 1

You will need: Paper; pen; sticky tape.

Write each word of the verse and the reference on a separate sheet of paper. Tape each paper to a child's back, telling them their word. Others can gently move children wearing words until they are standing in a line with the verse in the correct order. Repeat the words together several times.

Option 2

You will need: Crepe paper; scissors.

In advance: Cut crepe paper into streamers.

Space children out and give each one a streamer. Make a large, ongoing circle in the air with the streamer, saying the memory verse aloud.

Leader says: **God gives us his Word to guide and teach us. It is true for everyone, everywhere, at every time. It will never run out or need to be changed.**

Repeat the verse several times with children. Ask volunteers to make a circle and say the verse.

33

Memory Verse

The Lord is faithful to all his promises and loving towards all he has made.

Psalm 145:13

Theme: Faith

Methods: Activity; props

Option 1

You will need: Pot of bubbles and wand; paper; marker pen.

In advance: Write out the memory verse and reference.

Make two lines of children to face each other.

First group: **The Lord is faithful to all his promises,**

Second group: **and loving towards all he has made.**

All together: **Psalm 145:13**

Swap over. Repeat several times. Stand between the two lines and blow bubbles.

Leader says: **God's promises are not like bubbles that burst or fade away. They stay strong and firm, and God keeps every one of them.**

Option 2

You will need: A4 paper; marker pen.

In advance: Write one word of the memory verse and the reference on separate sheets of paper.

Starting at the bottom right with the reference, help children build up the memory verse like bricks from a base.

Repeat together from the beginning.

Leader says: **God promised King David that his son, Solomon, would build a temple where people could worship God. God kept his promise. God always keeps his promises.**

34

Memory Verse

Great is our Lord and mighty in power.

Psalm 147:5

Theme: Praise & Worship

Method: Movement

Place children in two lines, facing each other. First line shouts and stamps with great big steps: **Great is our Lord.** Second line shouts and stamps with great big steps: **And mighty in power.** All together, stamping with great big steps: **Psalm one forty-seven verse five**.

Repeat several times and then swap round.

35

Memory Verse

Blessed is he who is kind to the needy.

Proverbs 14:21

Theme: Christian Life

Methods: Movement; props

You will need: A long skipping rope.

Leader says: **'Blessed' means happy. When we love God, his love helps us share what we have with others. We are happy when we help God's family**.

Ask helpers to hold the ends of the skipping rope, and turn it. Demonstrate standing in the rope and skipping, or jumping in, saying the memory verse in rhythm as you skip. Give everyone a turn. When someone is tripped by the rope, allow them to continue from that point in the memory verse.

36

Memory Verse

A gentle answer turns away wrath, but a harsh word stirs up anger.

Proverbs 15:1

Theme: Christian Life

Method: Activity; props

You will need: Dictionaries, Bibles, cards, marker pen.

In advance: Write on the cards, 'gentle answer', 'wrath', 'harsh word', 'anger'.

Children with helpers can look up 'wrath' in the dictionaries. Choose four children to hold the cards.

While everyone reads the verse and reference aloud, 'gentle answer' stands in front of 'wrath,' who turns away. 'Harsh word' stands in front of 'anger', who spins round fast. Repeat with four more children.

37

Memory Verse, suitable for thick-skinned older children

Do you not know? Have you not heard? The Lord is the everlasting God, the Creator of the ends of the earth.

Isaiah 40:28

Theme: Praise & Worship

Method: Drama

Stand the children in a semi-circle, around one of the leaders, who faces each person in turn.

Leader says: **What is the memory verse?** The first child says the memory verse aloud. If they cannot remember it, or make a mistake, the leader rudely says: **You are the weakest link. Goodbye.** The child leaves the semi-circle. The leader turns to the next child, to see if they know, or if they have heard enough from the previous contender.

Eventually, everyone will be able to say the verse and reference from memory, having been put on the spot.

If you have particularly sensitive children, let the first two contenders be adult helpers, who deliberately make mistakes, and won't mind being told to leave.

Allow the children who are eliminated to rejoin the semi-circle in order to have another turn. By the time they have their next turn, they should have heard the verse correctly stated enough times to have remembered it themselves.

38

Jeremiah – God's man

Bible Story

Jeremiah 18:1–12; 37:1–40:6

Theme: Christian life

Methods: Props; puppets

You will need: Cardboard tubes; fabric; scissors; glue sticks; paper; wool; felt pens.

In advance: Make a Jeremiah puppet by sticking patterned paper or fabric around the lower half of a cardboard tube. Cut out a circle of paper and draw a sad face on it. Stick the face to the top half of the tube. Cut a square of fabric for a headdress and fix around the top of the tube with wool.

Operate the puppet with two fingers inside the tube and practise the script with plenty of interaction. After each question, have Jeremiah whisper his answer into your ear. Children can create their own Jeremiah puppets while you tell the story. Leader says: **Long ago in Bible times there was a man called Jeremiah. Jeremiah lived in Judah.** Show your puppet. **God gave Jeremiah a very difficult job. Judah had lots of kings. It was Jeremiah's job to tell each king, and God's people, that God was not pleased because they worshipped other gods. God had told them many times before that they were doing wrong, but they wouldn't listen.**

Jeremiah, how did you feel when God asked you to do this difficult job? Jeremiah whispers. **Jeremiah says he didn't want to do it, but God told him not to be afraid. God promised to tell him what to say, and to take care of him.**

What did the king and God's people do when you gave them God's messages? Jeremiah whispers. **Jeremiah says they still wouldn't listen. Once, they put him in prison for a long time. Another time, they put him down a well and left him there to die.**

How did you get out? Jeremiah whispers. **Jeremiah says that someone in the palace bravely asked the king's permission to get him out.**

What happened next? Jeremiah whispers. **Jeremiah says the king promised to listen to his message from God.**

What was God's message for the king? Jeremiah whispers. **Jeremiah says he told the king that enemies would come and attack Judah. God promised that if the king and his people gave in to their enemies, he would keep them safe.**

Did the king do what God said? Jeremiah whispers. **Jeremiah says that when their enemies came, the king wouldn't give in. He ran away, was captured and killed by their enemies. Most of God's people were taken far away to their enemies' country.**

What happened to you? Jeremiah whispers. **Jeremiah says that he was not taken away, but set free. He was**

very sad that the king and God's people hadn't done what God said.

Thank you Jeremiah, for telling us your story. It must have been a very hard time. Jeremiah whispers. **Jeremiah says he's glad he obeyed God. It's always best to do what God says, because God loves us and wants the very best for us.**

Remember

We have used the typographical shorthand of putting words the leader says to the children in **bold print**, and any suggested 'correct' answers to comprehension questions in *italic print* within brackets.

Instructions for actions or activities are presented in ordinary type either as part of the script or in a second column, opposite lines of spoken text.

39

Memory Verse

For I know the plans I have for you, declares the Lord.

Jeremiah 29:11

Theme: Faith

Method: Props

You will need: Several maps (local town plans or road maps, as well as an atlas) – one map for each pair of children.

To help children to learn the verse, recite it together several times while encouraging the children to look at the maps. Older children may try to work out a route from their home to a destination suitable for the type of map they have. If they have a street map, they should work out a route to the local hospital. If they are looking at a road map, they can find the way to a village a few miles away. Or if they have an atlas, they should seek a route to Manchester or Glasgow, whichever is more distant.

Once they have found the way to their destination, recite the verse again together. Ensure that the children understand that the word 'plan' doesn't just involve physical directions on a map, but also actions and good habits which help us move towards the goals God has for us.

40

Daniel & Nebuchadnezzar

Bible story
Daniel 1:1–21
Theme: Faith
Method: Music

Leader says:
The king of Babylon was called Nebuchadnezzar.
Help children say the name.

He was very powerful, and he wanted everyone to bow down and worship him.

But Daniel and his friends, who were taken captive into Babylon, refused to worship the king. They worshipped the one true God.

Sing this rhyme to the tune of *Baa, Baa, Black Sheep*, demonstrating the actions, and then repeat them with the children.
Yes sir, yes sir, oh, yes sir
Bow repeatedly.
Babylon's King, Nebuchadnezzar.
Make crown on head.
We have heard of your great fame
Walk up and down, proudly, chest puffed out.
People bowed down to your name.
Bow down low or curtsey.

But our God reigns forever
Raise hands.
And his power will vanish, never!
Flex arms and clench fists, bodybuilder-style.

Associated memory verse:
Do what is right and good in the Lord's sight.
Deuteronomy 6:18
Invite small groups of children to work together to make
up rhythmic chants using these words. Each group can
demonstrate, by which time everyone will have heard the
verse enough times to be able to remember it.

41

Daniel in the lion's den

Bible Story for younger children

Daniel 6:1–23

Theme: Christian Life

Method: Activity

You will need: A paper plate and craft stick for everyone; orange wool; glue; scissors; washable felt pens; sticky tape. In advance: Cut the wool into short lengths. Mark a simple lion's face on a paper plate. Spread glue around the edge of the plate and stick lengths of wool to it. Fix a craft stick to the back with sticky tape.

Help children copy your lion paper plate. Alternatively, lion faces can be drawn in advance, and children can fix the wool to the paper plates. Write children's names on the back of each plate. Talk about cat family members (cats, tigers, lions, etc.) and cat features e.g. paws, claws, teeth, whiskers, tails.

Leader says: **Daniel was good friends with the king, but Daniel loved God more than he loved the king. Some of the king's helpers didn't like Daniel.**

The king's helpers told the king that Daniel loved God more than he loved the king. The king's helpers bowed down very low to the king and said, 'Your majesty, Daniel talks to God lots of times every day. Daniel loves God more than he loves you.' The king

wanted everyone to love him most of all. **The king's helpers tricked him by making a law that anyone who didn't love him most of all must be put in a place with hungry lions. What do hungry lions sound like?** Cover your face with the mask, and roar. Children copy.

What do you think would happen to anyone who was put in a place with hungry lions? Children respond. **The king was upset because he liked Daniel, but he had to do what the law said. Daniel was taken to the hungry lions.** Cover your face with the mask, and roar. Children copy. **The king went away and left Daniel with the hungry lions.** Cover your face with the mask, and roar. Children copy.

The king was sad. Make a sad face. Children copy. **When the king went back, Daniel was still there with the hungry lions. The hungry lions hadn't hurt Daniel with their sharp teeth and claws. The king was very pleased to see Daniel and quickly took him away from the hungry lions. The lions were now very hungry indeed, and roaring loudly.** Place your mask over your face and roar. Children copy.

God was pleased that Daniel loved him more than anyone else. God kept Daniel safe from the hungry lions.

42

Memory Verse

The Lord is good, a refuge in time of trouble. He cares for those who trust in him.

Nahum 1:7

Theme: Christian Life

Method: Movement

Option 1

You will need: Newspapers, paper, marker pen, bin liner.

In advance: Scrunch up newspaper to make a pile of paper balls. Write out the words of the memory verse and reference on a flip chart or white board.

Read the words of the verse and the reference aloud, and then ask the children to join in as you repeat it. Invite children one by one to read from the visual prompt; as they do so, allow the others to throw the paper balls at them. Make sure everyone who wants to do so has a turn.

Option 2

In advance: Practise this with your helpers.

With everyone facing the back of the person in front, make a line or circle holding each other's shoulders. Cross left foot in front of right, then step with right foot; cross left foot behind right, then step with right foot. Repeat pattern. Don't concentrate so hard that you forget to say the memory verse and reference as you step!

43

Memory Verse

Jesus said, 'Go and make disciples of all nations'.

Matthew 28:19

Theme: Christian Life

Methods: Movement; props

You will need: A flag for each child; you may prefer to make these with the children. It is a good idea to have flags representing different nations – especially if your church has missionaries abroad or if you have other contacts with foriegn climes.

Stand everyone in a circle holding flags. Say the memory verse twice.

Leader says:

What does 'Go' mean? *(Go!)*

What does 'make disciples' mean? *(Teaching people to believe in Jesus and obey him.)*

Repeat the verse, turning around on *'Go'*. Take ten steps forward, holding flags in the air. Repeat.

44

Jesus asks Matthew to follow him

Bible Story

Matthew 9:9–13.

Theme: Christian Life

Method: Activity

You will need: Paper; card; circle templates; pen; tinfoil; scissors; bank bags; helper to take the part of Matthew; table.

In advance: Fill an A4 sheet of paper with different sized circles for coins. Photocopy onto thin card, one for each child. Cut and cover a set of coin shapes with foil, or use play money.

Show the coins you made and help children make a set of their own to keep in a bank bag. Leader says:

In Jesus' time, adults paid taxes to the government just like today. People didn't like paying taxes, but it was the law so they had no choice.

Matthew was a tax collector. He had a stall in the street where people paid their taxes. Many tax collectors cheated people by charging too much tax and kept the money for himself. No one liked Matthew, except other tax collectors. Introduce Matthew. **This is Matthew. It's time to pay your taxes. Let's see your angry faces and hear your grumbling as you hand over your tax money.**

Matthew: Taxes! Taxes! Pay your taxes here!

Children respond, giving their money bags to Matthew.

Jesus knew all about Matthew, but still cared for him. One day, Jesus went to Matthew's stall and said, 'Follow me!' Straight away, Matthew left his stall and went with Jesus to be one of his helpers.

Later, Jesus went to Matthew's house for dinner. Matthew had invited all his tax collector friends, who stole and cheated too. Matthew knew that Jesus cared about his friends. Priests and temple leaders were angry that Jesus was friendly with such bad people. Jesus wasn't worried what they thought. He said, 'I've come to get sinners to follow me. God's power can change them.' God's power certainly changed Matthew's life.

Associated memory verse:

The people were delighted with all the wonderful things he was doing.

Luke 13:17.

You will need: Paper; marker pen.

In advance: Write out each word of the memory verse on separate pieces of paper, preferably circular ones, to represent coins. Fold them up small and place in a bank bag.

Children can unfold the papers and put the memory verse and reference in the correct order. Repeat it together a few times.

45

Shepherds welcome Jesus, and celebrate.

Bible Story

Luke 2:1–20.

Theme: Christmas; Jesus

Method: Props

You will need: Two baby changing bags; baby essentials; shawl; rags; farm animals: sheep, donkey, cows, chickens; straw; picture of shepherds and angels.

In advance: In bag No. 1 put baby essentials and a shawl. Place the other items in bag No. 2.

Show the first bag and its contents.

Leader says: **New babies need so many things!** Children can share family experiences of what babies need. Using bag No. 2, invite volunteer children to find and remove the correct object from the bag as the story progresses.

Just at that time, everyone had to go to their family town or city to register their names, and be counted. Where does your family come from? Where would you have to go? Children respond.

Joseph and Mary went to Bethlehem. It was a long way, and almost time for Mary's baby to be born.

Bethlehem was full of travellers, and all the rooms were taken. A busy innkeeper finally let Joseph and

Mary stay in a stable cave. There were animals in the stable (Farm animals), and it wasn't very clean. Jesus was born there. He didn't have any nappies, clothes or warm shawl, just some bits of material. (Rags.) Mary wrapped Jesus up and he slept in the animal's feeding trough. (Straw.)

Outside Bethlehem, some shepherds were looking after sheep. (Sheep.) It was dark and quiet, but suddenly an angel in amazing light was shining down on them. He told them not to be afraid, because he had good news for them. The Saviour, the Messiah had been born in Bethlehem. The angel told the shepherds how to find Jesus, and then the whole sky was lit up with masses of angels, all praising God. (Picture.)

The shepherds were so thrilled, overcome, shocked and surprised that they left the sheep and went to find the baby.

Still full of angels, light, singing and wonderful news, they praised God and celebrated. They told everyone they met what they had seen and heard. This was the Saviour God had promised, and they had seen him!

Associated memory verse:
And we know that this man really is the Saviour of the world. John 4:42.

You will need: Paper; cellophane sweet wrappers; sticky tape; scissors; pen; reusable adhesive putty.

In advance: Write out each word of the memory verse and reference on separate pieces of paper.

What's the most exciting thing you've ever seen lighting up the night sky? *(Accept on-topic answers, hoping for such things as shooting star; comet; fireworks.)*

Children can stick cellophane sweet wrappers to a window, overlapping colours and filling the space. Help them stick the words in the correct order onto the window and read the verse and reference aloud together several times.

46

Memory Verse

Jesus grew in wisdom and stature, and in favour with God and men.

Luke 2:52

Theme: Jesus

Methods: Action; activity; movement

Option 1

You will need: Paper; pen; a Bible

In advance: Write out the memory verse and reference in lower case letters, beginning very small and finishing with very large letters. Write out the answers given in brackets below onto pieces of paper, and put them in your Bible.

Read the memory verse and reference together. Empty the answers from your Bible. Children can decide which is the right one for each question.

What do these phrases and words mean?

• **Jesus grew in wisdom** *(Jesus grew wiser or learned more.)*

• **Stature** *(Stronger and bigger.)*

• **In favour with God and men** *(God was pleased with him, and so were people.)*

Jesus grew wiser and learned more. Jesus grew stronger and bigger. As Jesus grew, God was pleased with him, and so were people.

How many people are in your family? As you call out different numbered-families, children with that number stand and say the memory verse.

Option 2
You will need: Paper; marker pens; sticky tape

Have children say the verse aloud as you write each word on a separate sheet of paper. Check their understanding of the words. Lay the papers in a hopscotch pattern, taping them to the floor. Demonstrate saying the verse aloud as you hop the hopscotch. Children can copy.

Option 3
Make a crouching circle. Touch eyes, ears, head.

Jesus grew in wisdom	Rise slowly
And in stature	Stand on tiptoe
And in favour with God	Raise arms
And men.	Link arms
Luke 2:52.	Mime open Bible

47

Jesus is tempted
Bible Story
Luke 4:1–13; Hebrews 2:18; 4:15.
Theme: Christian Life
Method: Props

You will need: Bottle of water; bowl of sand; branch; calendar; bread; stone; world map; three Bibles.

Hide everything except the Bibles around your meeting space. **There are seven things you might not expect to find here today. See if you can find them. Those finding each item can keep it for the appropriate time in the story, and hold it up.** Help three able readers find Deuteronomy 8:3; 6:13 and 6:16.

After Jesus was baptised in the River Jordan (water), **he went away by himself into the wilderness. The wilderness was mountainous, with rocks** (stone) **and sand** (sand). **There were few trees** (branch), **and no one lived there.**

Jesus stayed in the wilderness for forty days, praying and thinking about his special work for God. Have child with calendar count forty days from today and give the date. **Satan didn't want Jesus carrying out God's plan and tried to stop him by tempting him to do wrong. Satan said to Jesus, 'If you're the Son of God,**

tell this stone to become bread' (stone). **Jesus was hungry. He hadn't had anything to eat. He'd been too busy praying and listening to God. But Jesus knew the Scriptures, and told Satan:** Read Deuteronomy 8:3 (bread).

Satan knew God's plan meant Jesus would have to die, and that was not an easy thing to face. From high up, Satan showed Jesus far away countries (map). **Satan tempted Jesus by offering him an easier, but wrong way. Satan said, 'I have power over the world. Worship me and I'll give it to you.' Jesus knew that God's power is the greatest of all, and that God is the only one we should worship. Again, Jesus used the Scriptures.** Read from Deuteronomy 6:13.

Satan tried again, and said, 'If you jump off the top of the temple, you won't be hurt because Scripture says that God's angels will catch you. Then people will believe you're God's Son.'

Jesus knew this was not God's way for him. He remembered the Scriptures, and said: Read Deuteronomy 6:16. **Then Satan went away. Every time Jesus was tempted to sin, he didn't give in. He used the Bible to deal with Satan.**

Associated memory verse:
For the word of God is living and active.
Hebrews 4:12.
See idea 71.

48

Memory Verse

Forgive and you will be forgiven.

Luke 6:37

Theme: Christian Life

Method: Activity

You will need: Card; marker pen; paper; reusable self-adhesive putty.

In advance: Write out the memory verse and reference on separate cards.

Children can cover the paper with numbers. Leader says:

How many times does God forgive us when we do wrong? *(Too many to count.)*

How many times does God want us to forgive others? *(Too many to count.)*

Stick the memory verse cards to the paper. Read them aloud together. **God says he will forgive us if we forgive others.**

Repeat the verse, taking one card away each time until everyone can say it.

49

Jesus heals a crippled woman
Bible Story
Luke 13:10–17
Theme: Healing
Method: Puppets
You will need: Fabric; scissors; elastic bands; felt pens.
In advance: Cut two pieces of fabric for each child; one for
a headdress and one for a dress.

Wrap a piece of fabric around your index finger and secure
with an elastic band at the first joint. Use another elastic
band to secure another piece of fabric over the top of your
finger for a headdress. Leave space to draw a face later on
the front of your finger.

**In Bible times Jewish people celebrated the Sabbath
each week. The Sabbath was a day of rest, with time
to remember God and worship him together. Strict
rules kept people from working on the Sabbath.**

**One Sabbath, Jesus was teaching people about God
in the synagogue. Among those listening to Jesus were
the ruler of the synagogue, some clever teachers and
important people. They were not happy with what
Jesus said or did. They didn't like him being so popular
with ordinary people. They watched Jesus carefully,**

hoping to see him break their rules.

In the synagogue, Jesus saw a woman who was bent right over and who couldn't stand up straight. It must have been very hard for her to live like that. Show your index finger and bend it right over. Help children use fabric and elastic bands to create their own puppets.

Jesus called the woman to the front of the synagogue, and said, 'Woman, you're set free!' Jesus put his hands on her and immediately she stood up straight for the first time in eighteen years, and praised God out loud. I'm sure the synagogue was not a quiet place just then. Raise your index finger, and draw a happy face on it. Children copy.

The ruler of the synagogue was angry because Jesus had healed someone on the Sabbath. Healing was work, and was not allowed on the Sabbath. He stood up and said, 'There are six days for work. She should be healed on a working day, not on the Sabbath.'

Jesus said to the ruler of the synagogue, 'You all work on the Sabbath! Your animals have to be fed and watered. Satan has kept this woman bent over for eighteen years, God's special day is a great day for her to be set free!' The ruler of the synagogue and the clever teachers and important people were put in their place. But the ordinary people were delighted with what Jesus said, and the wonderful things he did.

50

Jesus, the Good Shepherd

Bible Story

Luke 15:1–7

Theme: Jesus

Method: Activity

You will need: Chairs; helper; tape recorder with recording facility and tape.

In advance: Have a helper practise reading this story aloud from *God's Story* by Karen Henley, (published by Kingsway) slowly and with plenty of expression. We reproduce it here for your convenience.

Lost and Found

Tax men and sinners came to hear Jesus. So the Jewish leaders and teachers said 'This man welcomes sinners. He even eats with them.'

Then Jesus told some stories.

'Suppose you're a shepherd. You have 100 sheep. But one of them gets lost. Wouldn't you leave the other 99 sheep out in the open? Wouldn't you look for the lost sheep until you found it?

'They you'd be so happy. You'd carry the sheep home on your shoulders. You'd call all your friends and neighbours. You'd say "Be glad with me! I found my lost sheep!"

'It's the same in heaven,' said Jesus.

'The angels are very happy about one sinner who is sorry. They're happy when one sinner turns to God. It's better than knowing 99 people who do what is right. Those people don't even need to say they're sorry.'

Make a circle with the chairs, leaving an opening. Sit everyone inside. Leader says:

**Jesus told several stories about being lost, and
we're going to hear one of them from the Bible. This
story is about a lost sheep. We all know what sound
sheep make. Let's make some sheep sounds together
to the tune, 'Baa, baa black sheep'.** Encourage everyone
to join in and record the noises on tape.

Have your helper sit in the sheep pen opening and read
the extract from *God's Story*. When the story is finished, play
the recording of the sheep noises for children to hear. **Can
you hear yourself?** Children respond. **Can you tell anyone else's voice?** Children respond.

**With lots of different voices it can get muddled and
noisy, and we can't always tell who's who. God loves
us so much that he sent Jesus as our Good Shepherd.
Jesus knows who we are and can tell us all apart from
each other. Only Jesus has the power to find and save
us from our sin. Only Jesus has the power to help us
change from doing wrong to doing right.**

Associated memory verse:
**The Son of Man came to seek and to save what was
lost.**
Luke 19:10
See idea 51

51

Memory Verse

The Son of Man came to seek and to save what was lost.

Luke 19:10

Theme: Salvation

Method: Activity; props

Option 1

You will need: Polystyrene chips or shredded newspaper, waste-paper basket, 14 blank flashcards.

In advance: Write one word of the memory verse and reference on each card and place separately in the money bags. Fill the waste-paper basket with polystyrene chips or shredded newspaper and bury the cards in it.

Let the children take turns to dig for buried treasure and find the cards. Read the memory verse out loud and let them lay out the cards on the floor in the right order.

Leader says:

Who is the Son of Man? *(Jesus.)*

What does it mean 'to seek'? *(To look for, to search.)*

How did Jesus 'save what was lost'? *(He came to rescue people who were lost in sin.)*

Each child can read the verse out loud.

Option 2

You will need: Wool; scissors; blanket.

In advance: Cut wool into short strands. Lay the blanket on the floor and 'write out' the memory verse on the blanket, using short strands of wool.

Read the memory verse several times with children. Invite a volunteer to remove several strands of wool. Repeat the memory verse. Continue inviting children to remove strands of wool and repeat the verse together until there is nothing left on the blanket. The number of children in the group will determine the number of strands to be removed each time. Repeat the verse one more time.

52

Jesus prays before he dies

Bible story

Luke 22:39–46

Theme: Jesus

Method: Actions; drama

Ask the children to play the part of the disciples, by lying down as if asleep. Read the story, bringing it to life by acting it out. If you have room to actually throw a stone, do so, and then kneel down in prayer. Ask another helper to play the part of an angel, and consider how to demonstrate the sweat falling to the ground. You may choose to use a dropper filled with water coloured with cochineal.

Leader says: **Jesus was willing to suffer and die on our behalf. That's how much he loves us. It cost him everything.**

53

Memory Verse

God so loved the world that he gave his one and only Son, that whoever believes in him shall not perish but have eternal life.

John 3:16

Theme: Jesus

Method: Action; props

Option 1

You will need: A world map

Place the map on the floor and stand with the children in a circle around it. Demonstrate the words and actions.

Leader says:

God	Point upwards
so loved	Cross arms over chest
the world	Join hands
that he gave his one and only Son	
	Rocking baby motion, release towards map
that whoever	Point to each other
believes in him	Hand on heart and head
shall not perish	Sink to floor
but have eternal life.	Stand up with arms raised

Practise until the children can join in the words and actions.

Option 2

Using a suitable instrumental track, lead the children in 'rapping' the words of this most famous verse.

Option 3

If you have access to a snare drum and someone who can play it, set up a marching tattoo and march around the room, chanting the verse in time.

Associated songs:

In the 16th verse

117 in *250 Songs for Children's Praise and Worship*

Recorded on *52 Scripture Songs with Ishmael* CHMCD006

Hallelujah My Father

75 in *250 Songs for Children's Praise and Worship*

Recorded on *The 500 series Vol 5* KMCD2432

54

Memory Verse

You are my friends if you do what I command.
John 15:14

Theme: Christian Life

Method: Activity

You will need: Scissors, sticky tape, paper.

Concertina the paper with five folds, and then cut out people shapes, joined at the hand and foot.

Unfold the concertina as you say together the memory verse. Colour the figures and write two words of each verse on their backs. Then fold up the concertina and continue to repeat the verse and reference aloud, from memory.

55

Memory Verse

You will receive power when the Holy Spirit comes on you.

Acts 1:8

Theme: Christian Life

Method: Actions

Recite the words and reference, using these accompanying actions to aid memory.

You will receive	Mime receiving a gift
power	Muscle-man posing
when the Holy Spirit	Link thumbs to mime a dove
comes on you.	Bring hands down sides of body
Acts 1:8	Hands make a book shape

Associated songs:

Hang on

77 in *250 Songs for Children's Praise and Worship*

Recorded on *Strike It Rich* Richard Hubbard SFC263 (tape)

56

Memory Verse

They devoted themselves to the apostles' teaching and to the fellowship, to the breaking of bread and to prayer.

Acts 2:42

Theme: Christian Life

Method: Action

Check their understanding of each phrase and then express the words in actions!

Apostles' teaching	Place hands as if reading a scroll
Fellowship	Place hands on the shoulders of the children next to them
Breaking of Bread	Pretend to hand bread to one another
Prayer	Fold hands, or kneel in prayer

Associated songs:

We believe in God the Father

223 in *250 Songs for Children's Praise and Worship*

Recorded on *The 500 series Vol 2* KMCD2372

57

Philip and the Ethiopian

Bible Story

Acts 8:4–8; 26–40.

Theme: Healing

Method: Music & rhythm

You will need: Paper; marker pen; reusable adhesive putty.
In advance: Write out the words of the rhyme and fix
where everyone can see it.

Sit everyone down and say the rhyme together, estab-
lishing the rhythm. Add the following sequence to the
words and rhythm: Stamp feet, slap legs, clap hands, click
fingers.

We are not the same
Since the Holy Spirit came.
We have power to tell and heal,
All in Jesus' Name.

Leader tells the story:

Jesus' friends waited in Jerusalem just like Jesus told
them to. God sent his Holy Spirit to give them his
power to tell others about Jesus and to show God's
power through healing and other miracles. The new
Christians met together to pray, praise God and share
what they had with each other.

Thousands of people believed that Jesus is the
Saviour from sin and the Christian church began. God

gave his Holy Spirit to them, too, with power to tell others about Jesus and to show God's power through healing and other miracles. Repeat the rhyme and actions together.

Jewish leaders tried to stop people becoming Christians and meeting together. Many Christians left Jerusalem and went to other places. One of those who left Jerusalem was Philip. He went to Samaria. He told people there about Jesus, and showed God's power through healing and other miracles. Repeat the rhyme and actions together.

While Philip was in Samaria, an angel told him to go out on a desert road. Philip didn't know what he was to do there, but he went. Along that road came a very important man from Ethiopia in north Africa. This man worked for the queen of Ethiopia and had been to Jerusalem to worship God.

He was on the long journey home in his chariot. He was reading the Jewish Scriptures. The Holy Spirit told Philip to go and listen. Philip knew something special was going to happen. Repeat the rhyme and actions together.

Philip ran up to the chariot and heard the man reading aloud about Jesus. Philip asked the man if he understood what he was reading. The man said, 'How can I understand unless someone explains it to me?' Philip didn't need telling twice! He was in that chariot faster than a streak of lightning! He knew that the

Holy Spirit was on the man's case. Repeat the rhyme and actions together.

The Holy Spirit gave Philip power to explain about Jesus the Saviour, and the man believed him and became a Christian. The man asked to be baptised in some water by the side of the road. So Philip baptised him. As they came out of the water, the Holy Spirit suddenly whisked Philip away to another town where people needed to hear about Jesus. The man from Ethiopia went home a completely changed man.

The Holy Spirit gave him power to tell people in Ethiopia about Jesus and to show God's power through healing and other miracles. And that was how the good news about Jesus spread and spread everywhere. Repeat the rhyme and actions together.

58

Memory Verse

Believe in the Lord Jesus, and you will be saved.

Acts 16:31

Theme: Salvation

Method: Drama

Put children into pairs. One child kneels down and covers eyes. Children standing (behind their kneeling partners) gently place one hand, palm down, on the head of their parner, and say the memory verse and reference. Children kneeling uncover eyes. Swap over until everyone can say it confidently together.

59

Memory Verse

For all have sinned and fall short of the glory of God.

Romans 3:23

Theme: What is God like?

Method: Actions

Leader says:

The word sin means 'to fall short', like an arrow failing to reach the target. When we sin, we fall short of God's glory.

Invite children to pretend to be archers, aiming for a target, releasing their arrows, but watching them fall short.

Say the words of the verse together, along with the reference, with suitable actions.

60

Memory Verse

You see, at just the right time, while we were still powerless, Christ died for the ungodly.

Romans 5:6

Theme: Salvation

Method: Action

Use actions, explaining 'powerless' and 'ungodly'. Help children find the verse in their Bibles.

You see Hands over eyes, like binoculars

At just the right time Stretch out hands like the hands of a clock, moving to the words

While we were still powerless Hold hands out and shrug shoulders

Christ died for the ungodly. Stretch out hands to make a cross then point to self

Romans 5:6 Hold hands out like a book

Leader says: **Why did Jesus have to die?** *(Jesus died for us. If we are sorry for the things we have done, he will forgive us and take our sins away. God loves us so much and wants us to be close to him, without any sin)*

Associated song:

You see at just the right time

248 in *250 Songs for Children's Praise and Worship*

Recorded on *Ishmael Praise 'n' Glories* SFCD264

61

Memory verse

We know that in all things God works for the good of those who love him.

Romans 8:28

Theme Faith

Method: Props; movement

You will need: 18 balloons, each with one word of the memory verse written on them (the reference takes two balloons – 'Romans' on one and '8:28' on the other).

Ask the children to take one balloon each, or more if you have fewer children than balloons. Then they will have to stand in a circle, so that the verse and reference are in the right order. Recite the verse together, and then burst the 'God' balloon, and repeat the verse despite the lack of visual prompt. Continue to burst one or two strategic balloons each time, pausing to recite the verse. Eventually, you will have no balloons left, but a roomful of children who know the verse by heart.

62

Memory Verse

Do not be overcome by evil, but overcome evil with good.

Romans 12:21

Theme: Christian Life

Method: Movement

Explain the meaning of 'to be overcome', which is to swoon or faint under pressure. Children will love pretending to faint!

Write the verse in full on a flip chart and encourage actions as you recite the verse and reference.

Do not	Shake head, wag finger
be overcome	Faint, falling to the ground dramatically
by evil	Stand up, make the thumbs down sign
but overcome	Faint again, even more dramatically!
evil	Stand up, thumbs down
with good.	Smile, thumbs up
Romans	Rub bridge of nose
12	One finger of left hand, two fingers of right hand
21	Two fingers of left hand, one finger of right hand.

63

Memory Verse

Serve one another in love

Galatians 5:13

Theme: Christian Life

Methods: Activity; movement; music; wordplay

Option 1

You will need: Paper; seven paper plates; a marker pen; scissors.

In advance: Make a paper banner, 'Believe in Jesus.' Write one of the following on the back of each of the paper plates:

Meet together

Encourage each other

Teach believers

Tell others about Jesus

Help others

Speak God's words – prophesy

Show love, with good deeds

On the front of five paper plates write one word of the memory verse, with the Bible reference on the other plates.

Make a seated circle, with the banner in the centre. Say the memory verse and reference aloud. Pass the plates around the circle, repeating the memory verse and reference aloud. Leader says: **God wants the church, his family, to stick** together and serve one another. **How can we do that?** Children turn over the plates and read the words aloud in turn. Pass them round again, repeating the verse.

Option 2

Make a line behind a helper. Have everyone hold the waist of the person in front. Beginning with the left foot, march on the spot in rhythm, saying the memory verse words and reference aloud.

When everyone is in step, the helper moves forward with everyone following. Make several attempts to get it right. Leader says: **We can only get it right when we all work together. Everyone's important. We are serving one another in love as we build God's church together.**

Option 3

You will need: Paper; marker pen; scissors; felt pens.
In advance: Write out the letters and numbers of the memory verse in large, outline writing, using a separate sheet of paper for each one.

Children can colour and pattern the letters and numbers of the memory verse and cut them out. They can pick up the memory verse letters and put them together in order, to make up the verse and reference. Make sure everyone is able to help. Leader says: **Everyone is important. God wants us to serve one another in love. We help to build his church as we love each other and give and share what we have together.**

64

Memory Verse for older children

The fruit of the Spirit is love, joy, peace, patience, kindness, goodness, faithfulness, gentleness and self-control.

Galatians 5:22-23

Theme: Christian Life

Method: Activity

You will need: Paper, marker pen, card, reusable adhesive putty.

In advance: Draw a large tree on the paper. Cut nine simple fruit shapes from card and write one fruit of the Spirit on each. Write out 'The fruit of the Spirit is' above the tree, and the reference on the trunk.

Read the verse from the Bible and children can stick fruit on the tree in order. Read the verse together. Remove fruit in order, repeating the verse each time until children are confident.

65

Memory Verse

Christ died for our sins.

1 Corinthians 15:3

Theme: Salvation

Method: Wordplay

Pin up or otherwise affix a large piece of paper to a wall or on a table top, and supply a pen to every child. Invite them to write, graffitti-style, several sins on the paper. You may prefer to discuss this first, gently steering the talk along the right lines. The idea of this activity is not to glorify sins, obviously, but to help the children to recognize that Jesus' sacrifice is sufficient to deal with all sins.

When the children have written (or drawn) their contributions to the wall of shame, then, using a marker pen, write the words of the memory verse in large letters over the sheet, along with the reference. Ask the children to recite the verse several times over.

66

Memory Verse

For God loves a cheerful giver.

2 Corinthians 9:7

Theme: Christian Life

Method: Activity; props

You will need: A box with chocolate coins inside (check for food allergies).

Sit with the children in a circle around the gold box. Say the memory verse to the child next to you. They can say it to the next child, and so on, until it arrives back to you. All repeat it together. Now open the box and share out the chocolate coins to eat.

67

Memory Verse

I can do everything through him who gives me strength.

Philippians 4:13

Theme: Faith

Methods: Action; wordplay

Option 1

I can do everything	Point to self, throw arms out
Through him who	Point up
Gives me strength.	Flex arm muscles
Philippians 4:13	Place hands as if holding a book.

Repeat together several times, with actions.

Option 2

You will need: Paper; marker pen.

In advance: Write out the verse and reference.

Make a circle. Say the first word. The person next to you says the first and second word. The third person says the first, second and third words. Continue until the verse is complete. Begin again with someone else.

Associated song:

I can do all things

97 in *250 Songs for Children's Praise and Worship*

Recorded on *We Are Kingdom Kids* Jim Bailey KMCD787

68

Memory Verse

My God will meet all your needs according to his glorious riches in Christ Jesus
Philippians 4:19

Theme: Jesus
Method: Activity

Option 1

You will need: Bibles.

Help children find Philippians 4:19. Read the verse slowly aloud together.

Leader says:

Everyone who has a sister say the memory verse with me.

Repeat with other groups e.g. brother, likes chips, is wearing blue, knows Jesus has God's power, etc.

This verse shows that whoever you are or whatever you need, God knows all about you, loves you completely and will meet all your needs with his mighty power in a way which makes it clear that he is in charge and gets the glory.

Option 2

You will need: Coloured paper; pen; Bibles.

In advance: Write out each word of the memory verse and reference on separate sheets of paper.

Children can try to put the verse in order. Help children look up the Bible verse to check it out. On completion, read the verse and reference aloud several times while one or two selected leaders jumble up the words to make it a test of memory, not just of reading.

69

Memory Verse

Devote yourselves to prayer, being watchful and thankful.

Colossians 4:2

Theme: Prayer; Christian Life

Methods: Activity; props

You will need: Nine paper hearts.

In advance: Write out each word of the verse on a separate heart, and the reference on the last one.

Scatter the hearts around the room. Invite the children to find the words and to put them in the right order. Explain that 'devote' means to give yourself, full of love. Then lead the children in these actions:

Devote yourselves	Cross hands over chest.
to prayer,	Lift hands to God.
being watchful	Make binoculars with hands.
and thankful.	Clap hands.
Colossians 4:2	Open hands as if holding Bible.

70

Memory Verse

Therefore encourage one another, and build each other up.

1 Thessalonians 5:11.

Theme: Christian Life

Methods: Action; activity; movement; wordplay

Option 1

You will need: Bibles.

Help children find the verse in their Bibles and repeat together several times. Explain how a human pyramid works. Build pyramids of three with plenty of help. Once built, repeat the verse together. Then explain that 'build each other up' means we should help one another to grow in our faith.

Option 2

You will need: Bibles; coloured paper; scissors; pens.

Jonah, for example, was on his own, without anyone to encourage him to obey God. We can encourage each other to obey God. Children can use the coloured paper to make ten simple fish shapes. They can find the Bible verse and write one word on each fish (including the reference), laying them in order. Repeat the verse together.

Option 3

Children can make a tower with their fists, one on top of another. Move the bottom fist to the top, with that child repeating one word of the verse and reference each time. Keep going!

Option 4

Leader says:

These words are in a letter Paul wrote to the church at Thessalonica. He wrote two letters to that church. Help children find 1 Thessalonians in their Bibles. **People at Thessalonica were called Thessalonians.** Make two teams.

Team A: Therefore encourage one another.

Team B: And build one another up

All together: 1 Thessalonians 5:11.

Swap over.

71

Memory Verse

For the word of God is living and active.
Hebrews 4:12

Theme: Christian Life
Methods: Action; movement

Option 1

You will need: Black and white crêpe paper; saucepan lids;
scissors.

In advance: Cut the crêpe paper into streamers.

Let the children experiment with swirling crêpe paper
streamers for smoke, crashing lids for thunder, and making
trumpet sounds with hands and mouths. Remind everyone
of the memory verse and repeat it together with actions
and sounds, very loudly.

Option 2

Leader says:

How do you know when something is living and
active? *(It moves, grows or works.)*
The Bible tells us that the word of God is living and
active. When God speaks to us, our understanding of
him grows, and he works in us so that we can love and
obey him.

Say the memory verse and reference aloud. Repeat slowly
together. Have children crouch down as seeds underground.

As you repeat the verse together, seeds can explode through the earth, stretching up high. Repeat several times.

Option 3
Spread everyone out well. Demonstrate action poses for boxing, judo, kung fu, fencing or sword fighting.
The Bible tells us that the Word of God is living and active. We can use it just like Jesus did to fight temptation, and win.

Repeat the memory verse and reference several times with actions.

72

Memory Verse

If any of you lacks wisdom, he should ask God, who gives generously to all.

James 1:5

Theme: Prayer

Method: Wordplay

Option 1

You will need: Bibles; paper; marker pen.

In advance: Write out the words of the memory verse and reference on separate sheets of paper, except the word 'wisdom'.

Muddle and spread the papers on the floor. Help everyone find James 1:5, reading it aloud together. Explain the word, 'lack'. Keep repeating the verse while the children put the papers in the right order. Explain why the word 'wisdom' is missing – if we lack it, God will supply it! Finally repeat aloud together from the assembled verse, several times.

Option 2

You will need: Paper; whiteboard; marker pen.

In advance: Write out the words of the verse and reference on separate pieces of paper. Muddle them up.

Choose several volunteers to stand in front of other children. Give each volunteer several words. Have a helper ready with the marker pen and whiteboard. On *1-2-3 Go!*

volunteer children all call out their words together. Other children listen and run to write the words they hear on the whiteboard. Helpers can write the words for children who need help. When all the words have been listed, children can try to put them in the correct order and read them aloud together

Leader says:

When we don't know the right thing to do, we can ask God. If we listen, he will tell us and help us do it. When we do know the right thing to do, what should we do? *(Do it!)* **Obeying God is the best way.**

73

Memory Verse

Cast all your anxiety on him because he cares for you.

1 Peter 5:7

Theme: Prayer

Methods: Activity; movement; props

You will need: Card; scissors; marker pen.

In advance: Cut out twelve stone shapes and write a word of the memory verse and reference on each one.

Option 1

Make a tight, seated circle with children and empty the cards over them. Help children sort out the words in order and read them aloud.

Option 2

Lay the cards on the floor in order like stepping stones. Step across the stepping stones memory verse cards, saying them aloud.

In turn, children copy.

Option 3

You will need: Washable red felt pen or red face paint; kitchen roll.

Pinch your first finger and thumb together on one hand and draw a mouth shape around them.

Leader says:

Sometimes it's hard to speak up and say what's right. We don't need to be anxious or afraid because God cares for us and will help us.

Move the 'mouth' up and down to 'speak' as you say the verse. Help children draw a mouth in the same way, and repeat the verse together.

Teaching the Bible to over-9s

This age group brings its own challenges and opportunities! Even at the younger end of the age range young people are beginning to show signs of the adolescent inconsistency, where they swing from the heights of maturity to the far reaches of childishness within minutes. My eleven year old daughter showed enormous concern for the fate of a well-loved soft toy as it went into the washing machine, whilst sneaking upstairs to paint her nails!

So within the group you may find that some activities which would seem to be 'beneath them' actually prove to be very popular and effective. Then at other times methods which seem to be in keeping with their stage of development do not engage anybody.

If the young people have been brought up in a church setting there is sometimes a tendency for them to feel that they 'know it all' about the Bible. Whether or not this has any truth in terms of familiarity with verses and stories, the challenge remains to deepen their experience of God speaking into their lives through his word. As they approach their teenage years, with their unique pressures and challenges it is vital that they are able to grasp the importance the Bible can have in shaping their outlook on life and coping with attitudes found in the world.

It is important to use a variety of methods and activities in your teaching in order cater for all the learning styles represented in your group. They may very well be at the stage where they are able to enjoy the wit of clever word play and can respond well to its use in the learning of verses; for example, when learning Psalm 40:1, 'I waited patiently for the Lord; he turned to me and heard my cry.' The dressing up of a child or leader in bandages as a 'patient' is a pun as well as a good visual prompt.

Reading and writing skills are on the whole well developed – although sensitivity still needs to be shown to those who struggle to keep up – and therefore these can be used more, both in the learning of verses and the reading of stories.

I have noticed how children are much more likely to give their full attention when one of their peers reads out loud than when a leader does, so take advantage of this! It is good when the story lends itself to this to use young people to read out the lines of different characters in order to give variety and to involve as many as possible.

Attention can be maintained by assigning various actions to particular words – an activity which works well for fives to nines but is also fun for older children.

Many of this age group enjoy performing – and are very keen to take part in acting out Bible stories, and devising their own ways of presenting verses. It helps to encourage them to give a performance, which will show if they have really understood the meaning and relevance of the scripture.

This group are intensely competitive. While we need to take care to underemphasize winning and losing, contests are always welcome – especially males versus females (not politically correct, but true)! You can use this to your advantage when asking your follow-up questions arising from a Bible reading. I was amazed on one occasion to see the enthusiasm shown by two teams to answer questions about the fall of Jericho, simply in order to remove a Duplo brick from their own wall – and there was no prize for the winners!

Don't forget to include art and craft activities in your teaching methods. Many of your group will respond well to this. Creating a collage or poster is a great way of enhancing the depth of understanding, as finding suitable illustrations or words helps young people think through the issues related to the Bible verse.

I am sure that the following suggestions will provide fun for your young people and that they help to foster within them a love for God's word.

74

Memory verse

In the beginning God created the heavens and the earth.

Genesis 1:1

Theme: What is God like?

Method: Actions

The first characteristic of God that the Bible teaches is that he is creative. This verse is a foundation stone on which young people may stand in a world which teaches them about evolutionary chance and meaninglessness.

Learn the words and reference by working with the young people to invent actions for the key words 'beginning', 'created', 'heavens', 'earth', 'Genesis'.

For example: 'beginning' – athletics starter's pistol; 'created' – mime working at a potter's wheel; 'heavens' – strum a harp (?); 'earth' – digging with a spade. Doubtless you (or your young people) can do better than this.

Repeat until memorized (which means everyone is saying the verse and reference confidently without any visual prompt).

75

Memory Verse

The Lord does not look at the things man looks at. Man looks at the outward appearance, but the Lord looks at the heart.

1 Samuel 16:7

Theme: God

Method: Actions

You will need: Doughnuts with various fillings, knife.

In advance: Disguise some of the doughnuts by smearing, for example, a tiny amount of jam on one of the custard-filled ones.

God spoke these words to Samuel when he was guiding him to choose a king for Israel. God can see what people are like on the inside, and obviously that's more important.

Ask the young people to guess the fillings of the doughnuts. Some will be easier to guess than others; some will have been disguised beforehand. Just because a doughnut has a smear of jam on the outside, for example, it may still be filled with custard or apple and cinnamon. In the same way, someone who has a spiritual appearance may not have a heart which is right with God. After each guess (or when the guess has been agreed upon by a majority), cut the doughnut open to reveal the filling.

Working in pairs, with one person representing 'the Lord' and the other 'man', ask the young people to create suitable actions to accompany the verse. For example: 'look' – mime binoculars or Sherlock Holmes' magnifying glass; 'outward appearance' – preen like a model on the cat-walk.

By the time they have done this, they should be able to recite the verse from memory. If not, repeat until this is achieved.

Then, having checked for allergies, consume the dough-nuts with vigour but without licking your lips, if you think you can.

Remember

We have used the typographical shorthand of putting words the leader says to the children in **bold print**, and any suggested 'correct' answers to comprehension questions in *italic print* within brackets.

Instructions for actions or activities are presented in ordinary type either as part of the script or in a second column, opposite lines of spoken text.

76

Memory Verse

How long will you waver between two opinions? If the Lord is God, follow him.

1 Kings 18:21

Theme: Christian Life

Methods: Actions; movement

Option 1

Using chalk or a length of masking tape, indicate a line down the middle of the room. Then ask young people to walk slowly along the line as if it were a tightrope suspended 300 metres above a piranha-infested pool, while they balance a heavy book on their heads. Some will be able to walk slowly with their head still, but may not stay on the line. Others will work hard to stay on the line, but when looking down, will drop the book. Some may decline the task, but one or two boys may get silly and deliberately try to take on the fish!

As someone walks on the line, ask others to read out the words and reference of the verse. You may wish to point out that the last thing a tightrope walker wants to do is to wobble or waver, but to aim for the other side and to go there directly.

Option 2

Use actions to learn this verse.

How long will you Create an action for 'long' such as looking at a watch and shaking it or measuring something which is three metres long

waver between two opinions Wobble on the spot or mime making a hard choice

If the Lord is God Stand still in 'worship pose'

follow him. Rush to the other side of the room

1 Kings 18:21 Use hand signals for the numbers, and crown yourself to represent 'Kings'

Repeat until exhausted.

77

Memory Verse

But the plans of the Lord stand firm forever.
Psalm 33:11
Theme: Christian Life
Method: Music

God does not forget what he has said. His words are true and trustworthy for ever.

Learn the verse in pairs, by making up a clapping or stamping rhythm that will fit with the words. Ask various pairs to demonstrate their rhythm to others. The idea is not to see which one is the best, as any which have helped the young people to say the verse from memory have been a success already.

78

Memory Verse

Turn from evil and do good, seek peace and pursue it.

Psalm 34:14

Theme: Christian life

Method: Movement

Try learning the verse by inviting everyone to stand up and face the same direction. As they say the first part of the verse, they should turn to face the other way, and as they say the second part, they should walk forward, so that they actively 'turn' and 'pursue'. Repeat as needed.

79

Memory Verse

I waited patiently for the Lord; he turned to me and heard my cry.

Psalm 40:1

Theme: Christian Life; Prayer

Method: Drama

God does not just set the time for things to happen and sit back, relax and wait for the divine alarm clock to go off. Rather, he appoints times and seasons, and teaches us to be patient by waiting for the times to come around. But this verse also shows that God listens to our impatient prayers and requests as well!

In the same way, our 'patient waiting' is not passive hanging about until God shows up; the psalmist cries out to God, which sounds like passionate, fervent prayer, at least.

Learn this verse by dressing up one young person as a patient with bandages, etc, and one as a Lord or judge, who turns and listens. With a powerful visual prompt like this, you cannot fail to remember the verse.

80

Memory Verse

Your word is a lamp to my feet and a light to my path.

Psalm 119:105

Theme: Bible

Method: Props

You will need: Torch, blackout.

This psalm is all about the value of God's word. The writer was devoted to following God's law. Imagine what it would be like to try to remain on a narrow path if it was really dark and you couldn't see a thing. You might easily stray off the path and end up going in the wrong direction or hurt yourself by falling or bumping into things.

If you had a torch, it would be easier to keep to the path, go the right way, and stay safe.

Learn this verse by darkening the room, if possible, and reading the verse while a volunteer shines a torch at a Bible, at their feet, and then at the ground in front of them at the appropriate times. After a few repetitions, it will be memorized.

Associated song:

Jesus, Jesus, Holy & Anointed One

132 in *250 Songs for Children's Praise and Worship*

Recorded on *The 500 Series Vol 1* KMCD2361

81

Memory Verse

Trust in the lord with all your heart and lean not on your own understanding; in all your ways acknowledge him and he will make your paths straight.

Proverbs 3:5–6

Themes: Faith; Christian life

Method: Movement

Create helpful mime movements to assist the memory (if any of the young people in your group have a knowledge of British Sign Language, this could help considerably). Alternatively, rely on puns for words such as 'lean' (not fatty) and 'ways' (tips the scales).

Continue to repeat the verse until it is lodged firmly, unshakably!

Associated song:

Trust in the Lord

216 in *250 Songs for Children's Praise and Worship*

Recorded on *Children's Praise & Worship 2* CHMCD015

82

Memory Verse

'For I know the plans I have for you,' declares the Lord, 'plans to prosper you and give you a hope and a future.'
Jeremiah 29:11
Theme: Christian Life
Method: Wordplay

This verse can be used to back up any teaching about commissioning.

Option 1
In advance, collect 26 balloons together, and write one word of the verse on each balloon, finishing with 'Jeremiah' and '29:11' the last two. Make boobytraps of three or four by putting a little water into 'know', 'have', 'prosper', and 'and', and some flour into 'plans'.

Blow up the balloons and ask each young person to take one balloon, or if you have more people than words in the verse, allow them to take more than one. Read out the words of the verse, and ask the young people to put the balloons in the right order, and stand in a circle, facing inwards. Instruct them to hold the balloons high above their heads so that everyone can see the words.

Then, using four dice (or, of course, two dice rolled twice each!), generate a number at random.

Starting wherever he likes, a leader then counts around the circle the number of balloons, and wisely, safely, but ruthlessly bursts the relevant balloon with a safety pin.

Repeat the words of the verse again and then burst another balloon. Continue until everyone is repeating the words and reference of the verse despite the missing balloons and lack of visual prompt. The idea of the activity is to learn the verse, obviously, but the fun of the balloon-bursting (and the danger of getting wet or floured) maintains the interest!

Option 2

Learn the verse by repeating it aloud several times, changing your accent after a few repeats. Try Oxford, Scouse, Cockney, Bradford, Swansea, Glaswegian and Geordie. A leader may need to demonstrate first.

83

Memory verse

And what does the Lord require of you? To act justly, to love mercy and to walk humbly with your God.

Micah 6:8

Theme: Christian Life

Method: Wordplay

Some memory verses contain this sort of list, which can be learned by associating the verse with a mental image to aid recall. In this case, we can help young people learn the order of requirements by using the initials of the three items.

Invite everyone to suggest creative and visual ways to help them remember the complicated parts of this verse. The more bizarre or vivid the imagery, the more likely we are to recall it when we need to do so. And if the images are linked to each other (in this example, all strangely-behaving animals or food items), then this again helps bring them to mind in the right order. If you prefer, develop this activity by supplying drawing materials for the young people to sketch cartoons of their wacky ideas.

Act **J**ustly	**A**lligator **J**uggling or **A**pple **J**uice
Love **M**ercy	**L**lamas on **M**otorbikes or **L**emon **M**eringue
Walk **H**umbly	**W**hales **H**angliding or **W**armed-up **H**aggis

84

Memory Verse

Love your neighbour as yourself.

Luke 10:27

Theme: Love

Methods: Actions; movement

Option 1

Learn the verse using actions for each or most of the words. If anyone in the group knows BSL, then they could teach everyone the correct signs for each word. Repeat until learned.

Option 2

Form a circle. Starting with the leader, say one word of the memory verse each, proceeding around the circle. Continue to get faster and faster, until the verse is being said fluidly, with no visual prompt, hesitation, repetition, deviation or snorting with laughter.

85

Memory Verse

Jesus replied 'What is impossible with men is possible with God.'

Luke 18:27

Theme: Miracles

Method: Music

Learn this verse and the reference by using the theme tune to *Mission: Impossible*. It doesn't fit particularly well, but a few repetitions should seal these words into the memory.

86

Memory Verse

For God so loved the world that he gave his one and only Son, that whoever believes in him shall not perish but have eternal life.
John 3:16

Themes: Jesus; Salvation
Method: Wordplay

Option 1

This is one of the best-known verses in the Bible, and so it should be! Many people will already know this verse, and this should provide impetus for reciting the verse together without a visual prompt from the start.

Option 2

Divide the young people into four groups. One says only words which begin with G, H or I, the second group says only words which have two or more syllables, and the third group says only words which end with the letter D, E, or F. The last group says the other words. Then a leader begins by saying the words of the memory verse, with various groups joining in when appropriate.

This form of activity is really only suitable when the verse is very familiar. Please note that 'God', 'gave' and 'have' qualify for both the GHI group and the DEF group simultaneously (shown overleaf in SMALL BOLD CAPITALS).

GHI Group	Multi-syllabic Group	DEF Group	all the rest
			For
GOD		**GOD**	so
		loved the world	that
he **GAVE**		**GAVE**	
his		one and	
	only		Son, that
	whoever believes		in
him			shall not
	perish		but
HAVE		**HAVE**	
	eternal	life.	John
		three	
	sixteen		

Obviously, once you've achieved this virtually impossible task, then change the assignment of the groups around and try again.

Associated songs:

In the 16th verse

117 in *250 Songs for Children's Praise and Worship*

Recorded on *52 Scripture songs with Ishmael* CHMCD006

Hallelujah My Father

75 in *250 Songs for Children's Praise and Worship*

Recorded on *Worship Songs: Songs of Fellowship for Kids* SFCD321

87

Memory Verse

I am the vine; you are the branches. If a man remains in me and I in him, he will bear much fruit; apart from me you can do nothing.
John 15:5

Theme: Christian life
Method: Activity

To learn this verse, think together of pictures, symbols or actions for as many of the words as possible. For example, 'much fruit' can be imagined as large bunches of grapes; 'apart' may be dramatized using a mime of unbolting a machine.

Recite the verse together using only the symbols and actions; and then continue with no visual prompt at all.

An alternative to mimes would be to draw pictures which provide the visual prompt.

88

Memory Verse

And we know that in all things God works for the good of those who love him, who have been called according to his purpose.

Romans 8:28

Themes: Faith; Christian life

Method: Activity

This verse is a good summary when teaching about difficult circumstances, such as when Paul was thrown into prison, which seems to have happened regularly. Despite apparent disasters, Paul rejoiced because God had a great purpose. In the case of his incarceration in Philippi, God had plans to save the jailer and his family.

Option 1

Learn the verse by repeating it again and again, but after a few times, change the accent. Try French (think Inspector Clouseau), German (und ve no zat in all zingz…), Welsh, upper-class twit (e-an dwenoh thah tinallthaings…), Somerset yokel, whisper, Klingon (d'ragh vak, togh gr'afftaurgh…), fax-machine screech.

Option 2

Repeat the verse aloud over and over, starting with a whisper and gradually getting louder until you are shouting.

Then whisper again, breathlessly, just allowing the noises of lips and tongues.

Option 3
Divide the verse into 'bite-sized' chunks and learn each part in turn until you can string it all together. For example, 'And we know that' can be said with various different inflections, emphasising 'And' (we also know); 'we' (not you or many others, but just us!); 'know' (certainty); 'that' (not this, or much else). 'In all things' demands, does it not, a Magnus Pike-style vastly expansive gesture of all-inclusiveness. Continue in the same vein.

Associated song:
I'm accepted
111 in *250 Songs for Children's Praise and Worship*
Recorded on *Worship Songs: Songs of Fellowship for Kids* SFCD321

89

Memory Verse

Never be lacking in zeal, but keep your spiritual fervour, serving the Lord.

Romans 12:11

Theme: Christian life

Method: Drama

Ask individuals to read the verse aloud with different attitudes and styles: quietly, loudly, happily, angrily, quickly, musically, dramatically, intimately, secretively, guiltily, etc. Decide together what style would be the most suitable: enthusiastically is probably the best! Repeat the verse together aloud with vast enthusiasm, without the visual prompt.

90

Memory Verse

Follow my example, as I follow the example of Christ.

1 Corinthians 11:1

Theme: Christian life

Method: Movement

Learn this verse by playing a game of *Simon Says*, and each time the actions are correctly followed, say aloud the verse and reference. After a few times, the memorisation will be complete.

Alternatively, divide the young people into same-gender pairs, facing one another, about a foot apart. Explain that one of each pair is a mirror, and must reflect the movements of their partner. This is not an easy activity, but is one much-loved by those who enjoy roleplay and drama activities. Suggest that everyone starts with simple, slow movements, and gradually build up the complexity and speed.

While the young people are silently reflecting one another, a leader can read out the words and reference of the verse. Then swap roles, so the reflectors have a chance to lead (once again starting with simple, slow movements). Read the verse a few more times, and then encourage the young people to say the words and reference while they are continuing with the activity.

91

Memory Verse

For as in Adam all die, so in Christ all will be made alive.

1 Corinthians 15:22

Themes: Salvation; Jesus; Christian life

Method: Drama

Leader says: **All who sin, all descended from Adam and Eve, will die like they did. But all who trust in Jesus and are adopted into God's family will, at the resurrection, live and be like Jesus.** Learn the verse by first discussing the symbolism of baptism by immersion.

We die to sin, are buried and then raised to life again through the power and activity of the Holy Spirit causing us to receive new life in Christ. Then act out a full immersion baptism, with someone being lowered ('die') and raised again ('alive'). In addition, ask others to act the parts of Adam (posing like a bodybuilder) and Christ (miming breaking bread and passing the cup).

Recite the verse and reference together, using the drama as a visual prompt.

92

Memory Verse

Therefore if anyone is in Christ he is a new creation; the old has gone, the new has come.
2 Corinthians 5:17

Themes: Salvation; Christian Life
Methods: Activity; prop

Option 1

Use young people as visual aids to help everyone learn the verse. Select the oldest in the group, and the one who has joined most recently to represent old and new respectively. Ask others to think of ways to depict other words. After repeating the verse aloud a few times, ask one or two young people to stop being a visual prompt, and eventually you'll be saying the verse from memory alone.

Option 2

Rather than using young people as examples of 'old' and 'new', show new and old versions of similar items. For example, an old style telephone and the latest mobile; or a wax 78rpm record and a mini disc or iPod; a ZX81 and a palmtop computer. Use these as visual prompts while you recite the verse together.

93

Memory Verse

God made him who had no sin to be sin for us, so that in him we might become the righteousness of God.

2 Corinthians 5:21

Theme: What is God like?

Method: Wordplay

This powerful theological statement needs some unpacking so that young people can grapple with the truth as they commit it to memory. Jesus became sin while he was on the cross; since he died in our place and took the punishment we deserve, we can now become the righteousness of God.

Try to obtain a conjuring trick where you can show a transformation from one thing to another. This may involve a bunch of flowers which disappears in a puff of smoke, for example, or a small plastic beaker of water which, when thrown into the air, becomes the Statue of Liberty. This can illustrate Christ, the perfect Son of God, becoming sin for us.

Repeat the verse a few times with a visual prompt, and then remove first the key words and finally all of the words and the reference, continuing to repeat the words from memory.

94

Memory Verse

My grace is sufficient for you, for my power is made perfect in weakness.

2 Corinthians 12:9

Theme: Christian life

Method: Wordplay

Display the words and reference on an overhead projector, white board or flip chart, and then remove or obscure key words one at a time and continue to repeat it. Eventually, you'll be saying it from memory.

Key words, and suggested order in which to remove them: Power, weakness, sufficient, grace, 12, perfect, Corinthians.

95

Memory Verse

In him and through faith in him we may approach God with freedom and confidence.
Ephesians 3:12
Theme: Salvation
Method: Movement

Discuss the meaning of the words 'freedom' and 'confidence'.

Then, with the words and reference of the verse displayed, repeat the verse several times, having created movements or actions for the key words. Make sure that the movement which goes with the word 'confidence' is bold.

For example, you may use the following actions:

In him   Open a door
and through faith in him

                                  Step through the 'doorway'
we may approach   Step forward again, flourishing
                                  your large, feathered hat
God   Bow down low
with freedom   Dance a jig (or a polka, in pairs)
and confidence.   Step forward once again,
                                  with laughter.

96

Memory Verse

For God did not give us a spirit of timidity, but a spirit of power, of love and of self-discipline.

2 Timothy 1:7

Theme: Christian Life

Methods: Action; activity

Option 1

Invite young people to work in pairs or threes to write a song entitled *No Timidity for Tim*, perhaps using a well-known tune or a pop song. Make sure there are plenty of actions, and they can consider writing an introduction which leads into the words of the Bible verse, or a chorus which explains the meaning of the Bible verse in their own words.

Allow time for performances, and ask everyone to join in with the actions (and with the words as well if the tune is sufficiently familiar).

Option 2

Ask everyone to think of alternative words and phrases which mean the same as 'timidity' (e.g. shyness, embarrassment, fear, lack of confidence) to help them fully grasp the meaning. God does not intend that we should be afraid of people or their reactions to what we say. Instead, the Holy

Spirit gives us love, power and self-discipline, or 'sound-mindedness'.

This discussion should start to implant the words of the verse into memories. Make up actions or sounds to help learn the verse.

97

Memory Verse

All Scripture is God-breathed and is useful for teaching, rebuking, correcting and training in righteousness, so that the man of God may be thoroughly equipped for every good work.
2 Timothy 3:16

Theme: Bible
Method: Wordplay

Option 1

Discuss the meaning of 'teaching,' 'rebuking,' 'correcting,' and 'training in righteousness.' Then learn the verse by reading it together and then asking volunteers to select five words to erase at a time. After six repetitions it should be committed to memory.

Option 2

If you enjoyed the balloon-bursting activity associated with Jeremiah 29:11 (idea 82) you may like to use the idea again with this verse.

Associated song:

If I try and read a little bit o' Bible every day
106 in *250 Songs for Children's Praise and Worship*
Recorded on *12 New Children's Praise Songs Volume 1*
CHMCD001

98

Memory Verse

Let us hold unswervingly to the hope we profess, for he who promised is faithful.

Hebrews 10:23

Theme: Christian life

Method: Action

'Hope' here refers to the certainty of eternal life for all who believe in Jesus. To profess something is to declare it or admit it. 'He who has promised is faithful' means that God's promises are totally trustworthy. 'Let us hold unswervingly' encourages us to believe, and not to doubt.

You may like to make up appropriate actions to illustrate the verse, along with tyre-screeching car noises and wild steering when you reach the word 'unswervingly'.

99

Memory Verse

If we confess our sins, God is faithful and just to forgive us our sins and to cleanse us from all unrighteousness.
1 John 1:9
Theme: What is God like?
Method: Wordplay

Write the words of this verse and the reference on a whiteboard or an overhead projector.

Ask the young people to take a few private moments to stop and consider if there are any sins they need to confess to the Lord. Remind them that there is no need to dredge up stuff from the past, but to ask God to reveal any attitudes or actions which are not honouring to him. Then they should make a note of these.

After a couple of minutes, point them to this wonderful truth, and ask them to write the words and reference of this memory verse over the piece of paper where they have been noting sins to confess. Then invite them to step forward, one by one, to drop their screwed-up piece of paper into a bin. Assure them that no-one will check the litter to see what they've been up to, but that this is a symbolic way of demonstrating their trust in the Lord that he has forgiven their sins.

Repeat the verse together a couple of times, and then select a word or two to erase, just as we are 'cleansed' from our sin. One of the important differences is that God remembers our sins no more, while we proactively commit the verse to memory!

100

Memory Verse

This is the confidence we have in approaching God, that if we ask anything according to his will, he hears us.

1 John 5:14

Themes: Prayer; Christian Life

Method: Wordplay

Write out this verse on an overhead projector, flip-chart or white board. Leave spaces where the words 'confidence', 'approaching', 'anything', 'hears' and 'John' should go. Ask the young people to guess what word should fill each space: leaving out the reference to ensure no-one just looks it up and cheats!

Once you have filled in the blanks with the right answers (you may need to prompt these if the young people are stumped) you may all repeat the verse and reference several times, with suitable confidence and volume (so that you can be heard).

Index 1: by Theme

What is God like?

Index 2: by Scripture Reference

New Testament

Matthew		
9:9-13	5-9s	44
28:19	5-9s	43

Luke		
2:1-7	3-5s	5
2:1-20	5-9s	45
2:52	5-9s	46
4:1-13	5-9s	47
6:37	5-9s	48
10:27	9+	84
13:10-17	5-9s	49
15:1-7	5-9s	50
17:11-19	3-5s	6
18:27	9+	85
19:10	5-9s	51
22:39-44	5-9s	52

John		
3:16	5-9s	53
3:16	9+	86
14:15	3-5s	7
15:14	5-9s	54
15:5	9+	87
20:1-18	3-5s	8
21:1-14	3-5s	9

Acts		
1:8	5-9s	55
2:42	5-9s	56
8:1-8	3-5s	11
8:4-8, 26-40	5-9s	57
10:38	3-5s	10
16:31	5-9s	58

Romans		
3:23	5-9s	59
5:6	5-9s	60
8:28	9+	88
8:28	5-9s	61
12:11	9+	89
12:21	5-9s	62

1 Corinthians		
11:1	9+	90
15:22	9+	91
15:3	5-9s	65

2 Corinthians		
5:17	9+	92
5:21	9+	93
9:7	5-9s	66
12:9	9+	94

Galatians		
4:4	3-5s	12
5:13	5-9s	63
5:22-23	5-9s	64

Ephesians		
3:12	9+	95

Philippians		
4:13	5-9s	67
4:19	5-9s	68

Colossians		
4:2	5-9s	69

1 Thessalonians		
5:11	5-9s	70
5:15	3-5s	13

2 Timothy		
1:7	9+	96

3:16	9+	97
Hebrews		
4:12	5-9s	71
10:23	9+	98
James		
1:5	5-9s	72
1 Peter		
5:7	5-9s	73
5:7	3-5s	14
1 John		
1:9	9+	99
4:8	3-5s	15
5:14	9+	10

GUIDE TO... series

**An easy-to-read series of training books,
to help you and your team of children's workers
gain Biblical insights and receive practical advice
on a range of essential topics**

*Children's Ministry Guide to
Dealing with Disruptive Children*
by Andy Back   ISBN 1842910337

Children's Ministry Guide to Storytelling
by Ruth Alliston   ISBN 1842910345

*Children's Ministry Guide to
Fun & Games for Active Learning*
by Jenny Brown   ISBN 1842910914

Children's Ministry Guide to Using Dance & Drama
by Ruth Alliston   ISBN 1842910922

Children's Ministry Guide to Tailored Teaching for 5-9s
by Sue Price   ISBN 1842910353

Children's Ministry Guide to Building a Team
by Andy Back   ISBN 1842910884

**available from your local Christian bookshop,
or in cases of difficulty, from www.childrensministry.co.uk**

CHILDREN'S MINISTRY

Resources

100 WORSHIP activities for children — CHRIS LEACH

100 INSTANT Children's Talks — SUE RELF — Just add faith and serve

100 INSTANT IDEAS FOR ALL-AGE WORSHIP — SUE RELF

100 CHILDREN'S CLUB activities — IAN DYER

100 SIMPLE BIBLE craft ideas for children — SUE PRICE

50 FIVE-MINUTE stories — A resource for teachers, children's workers and parents

50 LIFE-BUILDING stories for use in school, church and home — LYNDA NEILANDS

50 stories FOR SPECIAL OCCASIONS throughout the year — LYNDA NEILANDS

50 FUN-FILLED Family Activities by Ishmael — Discover the Bible with your children

100 CREATIVE PRAYER IDEAS for children — IAN DYER

50 Musical Activities for children — ALISON HEDGER

ENHANCING YOUR MINISTRY WITH CHILDREN